MEMORY, REASON, IMAGINATION

Memory
Reason
Imagination

A Quarter Century of Pell Grants

Edited by
Lawrence E. Gladieux
Bart Astor
Watson Scott Swail

College Entrance Examination Board, New York, 1998

Founded in 1900, the College Board is a not-for-profit educational association that supports academic preparation and transition to higher education for students around the world through the ongoing collaboration of its member schools, colleges, universities, educational systems, and organizations.

In all of its activities, the Board promotes equity through universal access to high standards of teaching and learning and sufficient financial resources so that every student has the opportunity to succeed in college and work.

The College Board champions—by means of superior research; curricular development; assessment; guidance, placement, and admission information; professional development; forums; policy analysis; and public outreach—educational excellence for all students.

Copies of this book may be ordered at $18.95 per copy from College Board Publications, Box 886, New York, NY 10101-0886, (800) 323-7155.

Library of Congress Catalog Card Number: 98-073992

International Standard Book Number: 0-87447-605-4

Printed in the United States of America.

Contents

Part III: Imagination

A Message from Former Senator Claiborne Pell

I am truly honored to be associated with a program that has provided more than 64 million grants to Americans in pursuit of a college education. In the 1998-99 academic year alone, almost four million deserving students will use these grants at their colleges of choice.

The success of the program, I believe, is in its simplicity. Namely, that no student with talent, drive, and desire should be denied the opportunity for a postsecondary education solely because of a lack of financial resources. The Pell Grant program establishes a direct relationship between the federal government and the student. It is this core partnership—the motivated student empowered with a financial lift from federal resources—that has enabled the program to survive the vagaries of Washington politics.

I deeply appreciate all that policymakers and the higher education community have done to maintain the program, and I was grateful to be able to attend the Twenty-Fifth Anniversary Pell Grant Conference organized by the College Board. I was especially moved by the statements of current and former Pell Grant recipients on how the program had helped change their lives.

A lively debate on the past, present, and future of these grants is a healthy and appropriate way to celebrate the program's vitality. I commend this book to our policymakers at the federal and state levels. But as you debate what might or should be done, I caution you to avoid introducing too many complexities in a never-ending effort to reach perfection. Perfection is always elusive and never as important as maintaining and strengthening political support.

So, to all who strive for broader educational opportunity in America, keep up the good work. And above all, keep the student at the center of your debate.

Foreword

A quarter century after the creation of Pell Grants, 150 educators and policymakers gathered at the U.S. Capitol in Washington, D.C., to evaluate the program's accomplishments and future. The gathering in November 1997, was at once a policy seminar, anniversary celebration, and tribute to the program's original congressional sponsor, former Senator Claiborne Pell of Rhode Island.

The College Board was honored to host the Twenty-Fifth Anniversary Pell Grant Conference. Now it is our privilege to publish this volume based on the conference.

Our nation—and especially the millions of Pell Grant recipients—owe former Senator Claiborne Pell and his contemporaries a debt of enormous gratitude. The Pell Grant, perhaps more than any undertaking since the GI Bill, has crossed the lines of gender and race to become the epitome of society's efforts to ensure the American dream through the accessibility of higher education.

The College Board is dedicated to the principle that no student should be denied access to college for lack of money. Our commitment to need-based financial aid dates back to the 1950s and the founding of the College Scholarship Service®. CSS® was created as an association within the College Board to help colleges award federal aid as fairly as possible on the basis of student and family need. We remain committed to that mission today. And the Pell Grant is a powerful ally in the work of removing financial barriers to educational opportunity.

The Pell Grant program belies the canard that all things governmental are ineffective. We know better, and we recognize the contribution this program continues to make toward maintaining fundamental values of fairness. Nathan Ambrose of Barbourville, Kentucky, says he is living proof that Pell Grants save lives. Speaking at the twenty-fifth anniversary conference, Nathan said, "My Pell Grant gave me the chance of a lifetime. The grant helped me move up and out of a life of poverty, and now I have the opportunity to give something back."

Fifteen leading education organizations joined in co-sponsoring the anniversary conference and helping to make this book possible. We greatly appreciate the support and cooperation of the following organizations:

National Council of Educational Opportunity Associations (NCEOA)

The Education Resources Institute (TERI)

United States Student Association (USSA)

American Association of Community Colleges (AACC)

American Association of State Colleges and Universities (AASCU)

American Association of University Women (AAUW)

American Council on Education (ACE)

The ASPIRA Association, Inc.

The College Fund/UNCF

Hispanic Association of Colleges and Universities (HACU)

National Association for Equal Opportunity in Higher Education (NAFEO)

National Association of Independent Colleges and Universities (NAICU)

National Association of State Universities and Land-Grant Colleges (NASULGC)

National Association of Student Financial Aid Administrators (NASFAA)

Public Broadcasting Service (PBS)

Many individuals helped bring about the conference and this publication. Lawrence Gladieux directed the project and, with Bart Astor and Scott Swail, edited the manuscript. Ginny Perrin oversaw the final editing and production of the book. John Phillips was extremely generous with his time, imagination, and ideas. Roberta Merchant-Stoutamire worked tirelessly on conference logistics. Michael Carr and Rodney Ferguson of the Widmeyer Baker Group helped with many aspects of the conference. Ermelinda Carvajal provided invaluable support in the editorial process.

Included in this book are photos capturing a small but important slice of our country's legislative history—the final session of the House-Senate conference committee that hammered out agreement on the 1972 legislation authorizing Basic Grants. Also included are photos from the 1997 anniversary conference. We thank Marty LaVor, former congressional staff aide and professional photographer, for taking the pictures and letting us use them.

Finally, I wish to thank the authors of commissioned papers, speakers, and all who attended and helped make the Twenty-Fifth Anniversary Pell Grant Conference an event to remember in our nation's capital (see Appendix for conference participants).

We hope this book contributes to greater understanding and support for the Pell Grant program, so that more students can develop their talents and realize their aspirations through higher education.

Donald M. Stewart
President, The College Board

Introduction

When Congress reauthorized the Higher Education Act in 1972, it created a Basic Educational Opportunity Grant to help low-income students go to college.

The program had a shaky beginning. Although its enactment was supported by the Nixon administration, Congress was nonetheless worried that the White House might block start-up of the Basic Grant program through a budget rescission. Student aid officials in the U.S. Office of Education were called before Senate and House staff and warned that under the new federal law, every nickel of the $122 million appropriation for the 1973–1974 school year would have to be spent or they could be put in jail! When these student aid officials were also warned that under that same federal law they could not spend a nickel more than the appropriation, they complained that their task "was a little like hitting a bullet with a bullet." What were they to do? Senator Pell's staff admonished, "either way, you better pack a bag."

No one went to jail, even though some of the appropriation did go unspent. In that first year, 176,000 students received grants of $50 to $450. Since then the program has awarded more than $100 billion to an estimated 30 million students to help them realize their aspirations for education beyond high school.[1]

Over the 25 years since it was enacted, the Basic Grant has at times been a political football between the executive branch and the Congress. It has been reshaped by successive reauthorizations of the Higher Education Act, and it has been consistently underfunded in the appropriations process. Yet, as Tom Wolanin writes in the historical review appearing here, the Pell Grant endures as the primary "symbol of the federal government's commitment to equal opportunity in higher education."

Along the way the program was renamed in honor of its principal sponsor in the Senate. Senator Pell has joked that this was done in the absence of a "Senator BEOG." His colleagues remember otherwise. Former Senator Tom Eagleton recalls that back in the 1970s no one particularly liked calling the program Basic Educational Opportunity Grants, or (worse) its acronym, BEOG. So he and Senator Edward Kennedy got together during the 1980 reauthorization and said, "Let's rename it for Claiborne." Today the name Pell crosses the lips of students, parents, high school counselors, application processors, and college admission, financial aid, and business officers millions of times a day.

ANTECEDENTS

The Pell Grant is a legacy of American egalitarianism. Its philosophical roots run deep in our history. But as Martin Kramer suggests here, the enactment of Pell Grants in 1972 also sprang from pragmatic ideas and experiences specific to the decades following World War II.

Powerful inspiration came from the success of the GI Bill, which had demonstrated to skeptics in both government and academia that higher education could and should serve a much wider segment of society. The education benefits of the GI Bill were expected to keep a few hundred thousand young adults out of the labor market and off the unemployment rolls. Instead, several million returning World War II servicemen used over $14 billion in tuition assistance and living stipends to finance postsecondary education or vocational training. And more than half of these beneficiaries— over two million men and women—attended colleges and universities. The GI Bill tapped a huge, unanticipated demand for collegiate education.[2]

Nothing in the history of American social policy has quite matched the spirit and scope of the original GI Bill and its investment in young adults as they started their careers and families. Most previous federal aid to higher education, like that provided under the Morrill Land-Grant Act of 1862, was directed to institutions. GI Bill benefits went to individuals. The model has sparked the political imagination ever since. In the early post-war period, there were various proposals for some kind of civilian counterpart to the GI Bill. In 1947, President Truman's Commission on Higher Education called for "a national system of scholarships."[3] However, most federal aid-to-education proposals ultimately failed in Congress in the 1950s and early 1960s, stymied by church-state and civil-rights controversies and fear of federal control of education.

Meanwhile, colleges and universities themselves sought to open their doors wider by awarding scholarship aid progressively on the basis of family ability to pay. Dean John Munro of Harvard and other college leaders advanced a set of consistent guidelines for analyzing the need of aid applicants to replace the various rules of thumb then used on campuses around the country. In 1954, 97 colleges founded the College Scholarship Service (CSS) of the College Board, which developed the

Parents Confidential Statement for collecting common information on family finances and producing estimates of need. The early CSS experience demonstrated that it was possible to devise generally accepted principles and procedures for awarding need-based aid. The new system drew a growing number of adherents, including not only colleges but also state scholarship programs that were getting off the ground in the 1950s. Thus, a widely recognized standard was now in place, ready for the federal government to use once it got around to enacting programs of need-tested assistance.

The Soviet launch of Sputnik justified limited federal student aid—in the name of national security. The National Defense Education Act of 1958 created low-interest loans for college students, with debt cancellation for those who became teachers. The bigger breakthrough came in the mid-1960s. Along with civil rights legislation and the Johnson administration's War on Poverty, the Higher Education Act of 1965 included the first explicit federal commitment to equalizing college opportunities regardless of an individual's financial circumstances. Title IV of the law authorized need-based grants along with outreach and academic support programs for disadvantaged students, a college work-study program to subsidize student employment based on need, and federally guaranteed loans to ease the cash-flow problems of middle-income students and their families.

Once established, the federal commitment to need-based student assistance attracted enduring bipartisan support. And it was with bipartisan support that Congress created the Basic Grant in 1972, rounding out the federal array of means-tested postsecondary student aid programs. While the concept and practice of need-based aid originated in the higher education community, by the 1970s the federal government had taken the lead and would soon become by far the largest supplier of help for students to pay the tuition and other costs of postsecondary attendance. The framers of the federal programs, in fact, envisioned the Basic Grant as a foundation for all student assistance, federal and non-federal. In effect, the 1972 legislation called for a loose federal-state-institutional partnership to equalize college opportunities, with Pell Grants as the cornerstone.

THE RECORD AND THE ISSUES

The Pell Grant was born in an era when people looked to the federal government for leadership in addressing social problems. On the heels of the historic civil rights and other social legislation of the 1960s, the Pell Grant was enacted with much idealism and hope in the persistent American quest for fairness and individual opportunity through education. A quarter century later, what has resulted?

Data to measure the outcomes are limited, and research to pinpoint the effectiveness of student aid, or Pell Grants in particular, is inconclusive. The early experience of the program was promising. The constant-dollar value of the Pell Grant was at its peak in the late 1970s, and college-going rates for low-income men and women increased substantially during this period. Other factors were surely at work that must be considered when evaluating the impact of the program: the value of some state scholarships surged in these years, and colleges were stepping up efforts to recruit disadvantaged and minority students. But at the very least we can say that the newly created Pell Grant reinforced whatever else was boosting participation rates and closing gaps in access to postsecondary education in those early years.

FIGURE 1.   *The Maximum Pell Grant as a Share of Cost of Attendance*

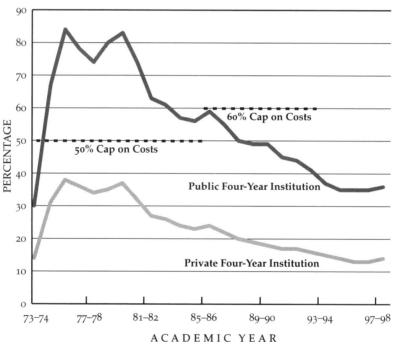

ACADEMIC YEAR

Source: College Board, *Trends in Student Aid: 1998.*

The 1980s and 90s, however, have been a different story, as the gradual extension of Pell eligibility to a wider population, rising college costs, and federal budget constraints have sharply limited the program's impact on low-income students. The Pell Grant has steadily lost purchasing power since the 1970s. As Figure 1 illustrates, its value has dwindled in relation to the cost of both public and private higher education. Recent congressional action has boosted the maximum Pell Grant by several hundred dollars, with the top award at $2,700 in 1997-98 and $3,000 in 1998-99. But the purchasing power of Pell Grants remains far below its peak of 20 years ago.

Meanwhile, the data suggest that the nation has been losing ground in the effort to equalize opportunities for higher education. As Mike McPherson and Morty Schapiro report, the rising net costs of college since 1980 appear to have restricted the postsecondary options of lower-income as well as African-American and Hispanic students. Overall, more students are attending college than ever, but the gaps in participation by race and income have been widening.

FIGURE 2. *Percent Share of Grants vs. Loans, 1980-81 to 1997-98*

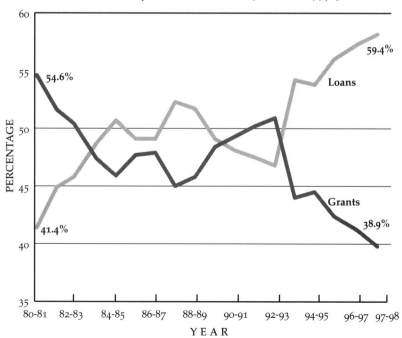

Source: College Board, *Trends in Student Aid: 1998.*

As the value of the Pell Grant has eroded, federally-sponsored borrowing for higher education has grown dramatically. Since the 1970s, student aid has drifted from a grant-based to a loan-based system (see Figure 2). In 1997-98, federal programs generated well over $30 billion in student and parent loans, more than five times the size of the Pell Grant program that was meant to be the system's foundation. Now, even those most at-risk must increasingly borrow to gain postsecondary access.

Much else has changed since the inauguration of Pell Grants. When originally enacted, the student aid programs and procedures under Title IV of the Higher Education Act were designed for families with dependent children who attend college full time. But today's postsecondary students are far different than they were 25 or 30 years ago. Growing numbers of students are beyond the traditional college-age group. Many more attend less than full time, and a significant number have family and work responsibilities while in school. Over the past two decades, the proportion of postsecondary students over the age of 25 has roughly doubled, from one-fifth to two-fifths of all students. Students qualifying as independent or self-supporting under federal rules now constitute a substantial majority of Pell Grant recipients (see Table 1).

Just as the recipients of Pell Grants have become more diverse, so have the objectives and the types of education and training programs supported by the program. Collegiate higher education is certainly what almost everyone had in mind when Congress first enacted Basic Grants and other aid programs under Title IV of the Higher Education Act. But over time, as Tony Carnevale and Lou Jacobson document, a considerably wider range of short-term, non-baccalaureate degree, and vocational training programs have been recognized and supported under Title IV.

Over time, too, issues of quality control and accountability in postsecondary education have influenced student aid policy debates, and there has been a growing concern that too many aid recipients (along with college students in general) do not complete their educational programs. Access has been the philosophical touchstone of federal student aid policy, with Pell Grants the leading edge of that policy. But in today's policy environment, as underscored by John Lee's chapter, student persistence to degree is at least as important. Getting students in the door is not enough to serve them well. Policy debates ought to focus as much on student success—degree completion in most cases—over the next quarter century, as they have on access for the past quarter century.

TABLE 1. *Description of Federal Pell Grant Awards from 1973-74 to 1997-98*

Year	Expenditures		Authorized Maximum Awards		Actual Maximum Awards		Actual Minimum Awards		Percent Cap on Costs	Number of Recipients	Percent of Recipients Independent
	Current	Constant	Current	Constant	Current	Constant	Current	Constant			
1973-74	48	165	1,400	4,857	452	1,568	50	173	50	176	13.3
1974-75	358	1,119	1,400	4,372	1,050	3,279	50	156	50	567	21.9
1975-76	926	2,701	1,400	4,083	1,400	4,083	200	583	50	1,217	29.8
1976-77	1,475	4,066	1,400	3,858	1,400	3,858	200	551	50	1,944	38.3
1977-78	1,524	3,936	1,800	4,648	1,400	3,615	200	516	50	2,011	38.5
1978-79	1,541	3,638	1,800	4,250	1,600	3,778	50	118	50	1,893	36.7
1979-80	2,357	4,911	1,800	3,750	1,800	3,750	200	417	50	2,538	33.8
1980-81	2,387	4,457	1,800	3,361	1,750	3,268	150	280	50	2,708	40.6
1981-82	2,300	3,952	1,900	3,265	1,670	2,870	120	206	50	2,709	41.9
1982-83	2,421	3,989	2,100	3,461	1,800	2,966	50	82	50	2,523	45.9
1983-84	2,797	4,445	2,300	3,655	1,800	2,860	200	318	50	2,759	47.5
1984-85	3,053	4,669	2,500	3,823	1,900	2,906	200	306	50	2,747	48.6
1985-86	3,597	5,347	2,600	3,865	2,100	3,121	200	297	60	2,813	50.4
1986-87	3,460	5,031	2,600	3,781	2,100	3,054	100	145	60	2,660	53.9
1987-88	3,754	5,242	2,300	3,211	2,100	2,932	200	279	60	2,882	57.5
1988-89	4,476	5,973	2,500	3,336	2,200	2,936	200	267	60	3,198	57.9
1989-90	4,778	6,086	2,700	3,439	2,300	2,930	200	255	60	3,322	59.0
1990-91	4,935	5,961	2,900	3,503	2,300	2,778	100	121	60	3,405	61.1
1991-92	5,793	6,779	3,100	3,628	2,400	2,809	200	234	60	3,781	61.5
1992-93	6,176	7,009	3,100	3,518	2,400	2,724	200	227	60	4,177	62.1
1993-94	5,654	6,255	3,700	4,093	2,300	2,544	400	442	–	3,743	59.2
1994-95	5,519	5,935	3,900	4,194	2,300	2,473	400	430	–	3,675	59.3
1995-96	5,472	5,728	4,100	4,292	2,340	2,450	400	419	–	3,612	58.5
1996-97	5,780	5,883	4,300	4,377	2,470	2,514	400	407	–	3,601	57.6
1997-98	6,256	6,256	4,500	4,500	2,700	2,700	400	400	–	3,683	56.6

Source: College Board, *Trends in Student Aid: 1998.*

Finally, the recent enactment of tuition tax benefits takes federal higher education policy into new, uncharted territory. Under the Taxpayer Relief Act of 1997, eligibility for the Hope, Lifetime Learning, and other education tax credits is being phased in over five years starting in 1998. No one yet knows how many taxpayers will benefit from these provisions, or exactly how much revenue will be lost to the Treasury as a result. But when fully phased in by the year 2002, the new tuition tax breaks are estimated to cost at least as much as the existing expenditure on Pell Grants and other need-based aid under the Higher Education Act. Many questions about the implementation and impact of the tax breaks are unresolved, including the extent to which they will over time compete with the traditional aid programs for scarce resources.

MEMORY, REASON, AND IMAGINATION

To consider these and other issues after 25 years of Pell Grants, the College Board and 15 co-sponsors hosted a conference on Capitol Hill in November of 1997. For two days, legislators, college leaders, and policy analysts contemplated the role of Pell Grants in assuring America's promise of educational opportunity for all its citizens (see Appendix for conference participants). Papers by leading experts were commissioned and presented to spark discussion. Our purpose was to celebrate as well as reflect on outcomes, to review what was intended and what has been achieved, to examine how policies have shifted over 25 years and what directions they should take in the next 25.

To structure the conference and now this book, we have borrowed a page from Thomas Jefferson. Many historians regard Jefferson as the father of American public higher education because of his authorship of the Northwest Ordinance of 1787 and his founding of the University of Virginia 42 years later. Jefferson's personal library was organized into three equal spheres: memory, reason, and imagination.

To refresh our collective **"memory,"** we first review how Pell Grants got started, what was intended, and the pathway this program has taken in its 25-year history. Part I of the book presents two retrospectives on the origins of Pell Grants. Tom Wolanin traces the legislative history of the program and the controversies it has weathered. Martin Kramer probes the intent of the framers and reminds us that in its conception the program was about motivating students to plan and prepare academically for college as well as financing it.

Through **"reason,"** we examine how the program has delivered on the original intent—its reach and impact. Part II of the book considers the results, foreseen and unforeseen, for students, institutions, and society. Sarah Turner finds that the Pell Grant has influenced institutional tuition and aid policies in unexpected ways, including a reduction of college costs for students of moderate financial means, not just those specifically targeted by Pell. John Lee examines the extent to which Pell Grants may have helped students persist to degree, rather than just gain access to college, and he suggests modifications to the program to increase persistence rates. Tony Carnevale and Lou Jacobson put a spotlight on the unheralded but critical role of Pell Grants in short-term job training for dislocated workers, welfare recipients, and other disadvantaged citizens.

Then we let our **"imagination"** roam into the future, exploring how government can best help close gaps in educational opportunity and meet the country's needs over the next quarter century. Part III of the book starts with Sam Kipp's profile of the coming, increasingly diverse generation of potential undergraduate students. His analysis suggests that our society and policymakers will face a daunting challenge heading into the next century, both in preparing the new students for college-level work and assuring that they have sufficient Pell Grants and other financial aid to pay the costs. The next two chapters present proposals for reconfiguring federal higher education policy. Arthur Hauptman argues that Pell Grants are a necessary but not sufficient strategy to raise the aspirations and performance of low-income and minority students. He recommends complementary strategies of early intervention and awareness of college opportunities. Mike McPherson and Morty Schapiro call for a new federal grant program that would piggy-back on Pell and give colleges a stronger incentive to meet the needs of lower-income students.

An Afterword offers reflections and themes drawn from the papers as well as the conference discussion.

The effects of the Pell Grant are intertwined with those of other public and institutional policies in a dynamic, interactive market for postsecondary education. This book thus raises as many questions as it answers about the Pell Grant program. In so doing, we hope it will contribute to more informed debate about a complex program and more effective national strategies for equalizing educational opportunity in America.

Lawrence E. Gladieux
Executive Director for Policy Analysis, The College Board

NOTES

1. See Table 1. The figure of more than $100 billion awarded is in constant 1997 dollars. The estimate of 30 million students having benefited is extrapolated from the cumulative number of recipients, which includes students who receive grants in more than one year.
2. See Michael J. Bennett, *When Dreams Came True: The GI Bill and the Making of Modern America* (Washington, D.C.: Brassey's, Inc., 1996).
3. *Higher Education for American Democracy,* A Report of the President's Commission on Higher Education (Washington, D.C., December 1947).

Memory

The original Basic Educational Opportunity Grant was born out of a Democratic Congress with support from a Republican Administration. The premise of the program was that every student with the academic wherewithal to go to college should be provided that opportunity—regardless of financial need.

In the past quarter century, approximately 30 million students have attended some form of postsecondary education with the aid of a Pell Grant. But the strength of the program can be found in more than the financial boost it gives students. It was also intended as a mechanism to spark the motivation, desire, and sense of possibility among disadvantaged students that they could go to college. Vision is often lost in the details. But the Pell Grant aimed to increase opportunity for low-income students and families by changing the mindset of our young people. With effort and the right preparation, they could make it to college.

Questions about the original vision of the Pell Grant, as well as how it should be altered to fit into the current mosaic of financial aid programs, remain on the minds of policymakers and educators. This section of the book, "Memory," provides perspectives on the evolution of the program that continues to help so many students today.

Pell Grants:
A 25-Year History

Thomas R. Wolanin

Abstract. *The Pell Grant program was born in controversy and continues to be surrounded by controversy to this day. Should federal aid for higher education be channeled to students or institutions? Should Pell Grants be targeted to students from the lowest-income families or be available to a broader group from moderate-income families as well? How should Pell Grants be distributed among the sectors of postsecondary education? Should Pell Grants be tilted toward traditional students whose parents help pay for their education or more toward self-supporting students? Should a student's financial need and size of award be determined by federal statute, regulation, recommendations from higher education institutions, or a combination of these? Should the Pell Grant become an entitlement program? The program has weathered debate on these and other policy questions for 25 years, and there has never been a serious effort to repeal the program. The Pell Grant endures as the symbol of the federal government's commitment to equalizing college opportunities. The challenge for the future is how to restore the Pell Grant as the real foundation, and not just the symbol, of equal educational opportunity.*

Two factors were critical to enactment of the Pell Grant in 1972. The first was the temper of the times, which supported federal efforts on behalf of equal educational opportunity. The second was the conviction and tenacity of the senior senator from Rhode Island, Claiborne Pell.

BROAD SUPPORT FOR THE CONCEPT

The 1960s provided the fertile soil in which an idea like the Pell Grants could take root. The dominant argument for broadening educational opportunity was social equity. Going to college was increasingly seen as "the primary means of moving into the mainstream of American economic and social life."[1] The companion argument was that enabling students to attend college who otherwise could not afford it served the national economic interest. By developing their talents and abilities and becoming more productive than they would have been without higher education, these students would contribute to a bigger economic pie for all. Such broad national benefits—greater social justice and economic productivity—justified taxpayer support of basic access to higher education for all who could benefit from it.[2]

Many saw the post-World War II GI Bill as the model for a federal program to expand educational opportunity. The GI Bill, with its generous coverage of direct educational expenses and living allowance, was perceived to have accelerated the mobility of veterans into the middle class and to have fueled rapid economic growth and prosperity. Among those who hoped to create a GI Bill for all students was Senator Wayne Morse (D-OR), who chaired the Senate Education Subcommittee during most of the 1960s and was succeeded as chairman by Senator Pell in 1969.[3] The legacy of the GI Bill and of Senator Morse was one tributary leading to the policy consensus in support of equal educational opportunity in higher education.

Another tributary was the War on Poverty of the 1960s, which focused domestic public policy on helping improve the opportunities of low-income Americans. The Office of Economic Opportunity, the lead federal agency in the War on Poverty, initiated many programs to increase the access of the poor to quality educational opportunities at all levels, including College Work-Study and Upward Bound, which focused on higher education.

In his message to Congress proposing the Higher Education Act (HEA) of 1965, entitled "Toward Full Educational Opportunity," President Johnson said, "[W]e need to do more . . . to extend the opportunity for higher education more broadly among lower and middle income families."[4] Upon signing the legislation, he declared, "[this act] means that a high school senior anywhere in this great land of ours can apply to any college or any university in any of the 50 states and not be turned away because his family is poor."[5]

In the waning months of the Johnson administration, Alice Rivlin, the assistant secretary for Planning and Evaluation in the Department of Health, Education, and Welfare, oversaw the production of a report, *Toward a Long-Range Plan for Federal Financial Support of Higher Education,* which focused on achieving equal educational opportunity through student aid. In 1969, the new Republican administration continued to support the idea of student financial aid as a strategy to attain equal educational opportunity. In his March 19, 1970, "Special Message to Congress on Higher Education," President Nixon said, "No qualified student who wants to go to college should be barred by lack of money . . . *Equal educational opportunity,* which has long been a goal, must now become a reality for every young person in the United States, whatever his economic circumstances."[6] The Nixon administration proposed a guaranteed basic level of assistance for all students that would "assure that Federal funds go first, and in the largest amounts, to the neediest students, in order to place them on an equal footing with students from higher-income families."[7]

Meanwhile, in the private sector, the Carnegie Commission on Higher Education issued a report in late 1968 setting out its basic views on federal policy for higher education. In *Quality and Equality: New Levels of Federal Responsibility for Higher Education,* the commission called for a major expansion of federal student aid as the principal strategy for funding access to higher education.

SENATOR PELL'S CONTRIBUTION

All the ideas for expanding federal student financial aid programs to advance equal educational opportunity in higher education could have easily joined the legion of policy foundlings that pack Washington bookshelves. It was Senator Pell, from his strategic position as chairman of the Education Subcommittee, who supplied the initiative and had the perseverance to distill these ideas and move them through the legislative process to enactment.[8] Senator Pell was the catalyst. He took advantage of a policy environment sympathetic to equal educational opportunity to produce a landmark program.

In the spring of 1969, Senator Pell introduced a bill to amend the HEA. His statement explaining the bill harkened back to the GI Bill, cited the Carnegie and Rivlin reports, and argued that broader opportunities for higher education provided social and economic benefits to the nation. He concluded that "there is almost total agreement that some kind of postsecondary educational opportunity should be available to all who desire it. Some would argue further that such opportunity should be a matter of right, and that making the opportunity available is a public obligation. I would support such a philosophic approach."[9]

While on a skiing vacation in Switzerland, Senator Pell had puzzled over how to guarantee all students a base amount of assistance to go to college while also making the grant sensitive to financial need, thus providing more money to those from the lowest-income families. The solution came to him while skiing down a mountain, and he jotted it down on a placemat in the ski lodge. His idea was to establish a fixed grant amount for everyone, but subtract from it the amount of income taxes paid by either the student or the student's family. This subtraction of income taxes would provide a simple way of reducing the grant to take into account the family's ability to pay. All students would know the base amount they were guaranteed to receive, but the largest actual grants would go to the lowest-income students.

When the actual bill took shape, it called for a "Basic Educational Opportunity Grant" of $1,200, minus the amount of income tax paid by the student or the student's family, available for each of four years of undergraduate study. The bill also retained the existing federal campus-based aid programs, renaming the Educational Opportunity Grant the Supplementary Educational Opportunity Grant, and authorized a "cost-of-education" allowance for institutions of higher education for each student they enrolled who received either a Basic or Supplementary Educational Opportunity Grant.

THE 1972 REAUTHORIZATION OF THE HEA: STUDENT AID VERSUS INSTITUTIONAL AID

Senator Pell's efforts were bolstered from two directions. First, the recommendations of the Nixon administration for the reauthorization of the HEA focused on expanding equal educational opportunity through a revised student aid program that guaranteed every student a basic level of assistance. Second, the ranking minority member of the subcommittee, Senator Winston Prouty (R-VT), favored a "GI Bill for everybody someday" and the "concept of a minimum floor of assistance."[10]

During the consideration of the reauthorization of the HEA in the Senate in 1971, Senator Pell's proposal was adopted with only two significant modifications. First, the amount of federal income taxes paid as an indicator of ability to pay was replaced by an "expected family contribution" to be established annually by regulation. Second, the size of a student's Basic Educational Opportunity Grant was limited to not more than one-half the cost of attendance at the institution the student would be attending. This provision was intended to ensure that no student got a free ride with grant assistance. Limiting the grant to one-half the cost was also an attempt to create a measure of neutrality between lower-priced public institutions and higher-priced private ones. No student could pay all the costs at any institution with a Pell Grant alone.

While the Senate was adopting the Pell Grant with little controversy, the House Subcommittee on Postsecondary Education, under the leadership of Representative Edith Green (D-OR), narrowly adopted and guided through the House a reauthorization of the HEA. The bill featured grants to institutions largely based on enrollments (capitation grants), rather than Senator Pell's direct grants to students. In a long and bitterly contentious House-Senate conference committee, the Senate strategy of focusing on student aid to attain equal educational opportunity prevailed over the House provisions emphasizing institutional aid.

The critical elements of the new Pell Grant were:

- It was in the form of a voucher awarded directly to students, who could use it at the institution of their choice. This voucher system would require institutions to compete for students in the marketplace, thereby, in the words of President Nixon, making them "more responsive to student needs."[11] This feature of the program was particularly important to the administration and the Republicans in Congress.

- It was based on financial need that targeted most of its benefits at students from lower-income families. This feature was particularly important to congressional Democrats.

- It was a grant that, while targeted to lower-income students, also made some aid available to students from middle-income families.[12]

- It guaranteed a measure of certainty. As an "entitlement," it would enable students who might not otherwise do so to aspire to higher education, secure in the knowledge that a base amount of funding would be available to them.

- It was expressed in terms of a fixed maximum amount, again to better inform students of the amount of money guaranteed to them.

- It guaranteed all students access to higher education but also provided for a measure of choice among types of institutions, particularly through the half-cost provision.

- It was an add-on to the existing campus-based aid programs rather than a replacement.

- It was a mechanism for assisting institutions—through cost-of-education allowances—based on their enrollment of federally aided students.

The Office of Education, a division of the Department of Health, Education, and Welfare and the predecessor of the current Department of Education, moved quickly and energetically to get the new program up and running. Funding limitations and administrative difficulties, however, slowed the launch. The Pell Grant was phased in one class at a time beginning with freshmen in the 1973-74 academic year, and was initially limited to full-time students. As the process of reauthorizing the HEA in 1976 began, the Pell Grant program was barely off the ground.

THE 1976 REAUTHORIZATION: ACCESS AND CHOICE

The new chairman of the House Subcommittee on Postsecondary Education, Congressman James G. O'Hara (D-MI) was committed to continuing the Pell Grant program, but he targeted the half-cost provision for elimination. O'Hara reasoned that it was unfair to deny the lowest-income students, who were eligible for the largest Pell Grants, their full awards to attend a low-cost community college to enhance the relative competitive position of the higher-priced private colleges. It was also difficult to find any evidence that the half-cost provision in fact provided any real benefit to private colleges, while its harm to the lowest-income students attending the lowest-cost colleges was quite evident. Nevertheless, the half-cost provision had come to represent the federal government's concern for private higher education, particularly for the less-competitive, financially struggling private institutions. The private colleges fiercely and successfully resisted the repeal of the half-cost provision until 1992.

The requirement that the existing federal campus-based programs be funded at least at current levels before funds were provided for the new Pell Grant was also of special importance to the private colleges. The campus-based programs permitted private colleges to construct a package of student aid on the Pell Grant foundation that enabled students to choose more expensive postsecondary educational alternatives. The 1976 reauthorization retained this threshold or trigger provision, but it was repealed in the 1986 reauthorization, by which time it had become clear that the campus-based programs could stand on their own political feet. More important, it was obvious that the appropriations committees routinely ignored these triggers, which served mainly to irritate the appropriators rather than to constrain their behavior. By the early 1990s, while choice among postsecondary institutions remained an objective of the overall federal student aid system, it was no longer an identifiable mission of the Pell Grant.

Aside from the fight over the half-cost provision in the House, the 1976 reauthorization of the HEA proceeded smoothly. The Pell Grant program was extended through the 1979-80 academic year, and the authorized maximum grant was increased from $1,400 to $1,800. The 1976 reauthorization of the HEA focused on changes in the Guaranteed Student Loan Program aimed at ensuring adequate participation by banks and other lenders and curbing defaults by student borrowers.[13]

THE MIDDLE INCOME STUDENT ASSISTANCE ACT OF 1978

In the late 1970s, concern about the burden of college costs for middle-income families generated legislative proposals for tuition tax credits. The Carter administration (1977–1981) and its allies in Congress were adamantly opposed to such tax breaks. In addition to threatening to veto such legislation, the administration produced an alternative, the Middle Income Student Assistance Act (MISAA). The bill dramatically expanded the availability of Pell Grants to students from middle-income families by reducing the assessment rate on discretionary income in the formula for determining the expected family contribution. MISAA also made all students, regardless of family income, eligible for the in-school interest subsidy offered by the Guaranteed Student Loan Program.

MISAA was one major chapter in the ongoing debate over the degree to which Pell Grants should be heavily targeted to students from the lowest-income families or made available to students from both moderate- and low-income families. As adopted in 1972, Pell Grants were intended, in the words of Senator Pell, to "aid those in the lowest-income groups the most, while making some assistance available at the middle-income level."[14] The law provided for the administration to publish an annual "schedule of expected family contributions," which effectively determined the targeting of Pell Grants by family income category. Understanding full well the importance of the schedule of expected family contributions in determining who would benefit from the Pell Grant program, Congress provided in the 1972 act for this schedule to be subject to disapproval through a legislative veto. Through the 1970s, the executive branch generally proposed targeting Pell Grants more toward students from low-income families to restrain program costs and to use scarce federal tax dollars most efficiently, while Congress tended toward serving more of its constituents with a less-targeted program.

The Pell Grant program as enacted in 1972 also contained a provision to reduce student awards in the event that appropriations were not sufficient to make all the awards at the level established by the statutory maximum. This "reduction formula" gave another clear illustration of congressional intent with respect to the targeting of Pell Grants. The formula aimed to achieve two goals: first, to provide the largest amount of funding for students from the lowest-income families and second, to keep as many students as possible in the program. Therefore, the formula provided that if full funding was not available, students eligible for the largest awards (i.e., those from the lowest-income families) would have their awards reduced the least. Those eligible for the smallest awards would have their awards reduced the most, but they would not be eliminated from the program unless their grants shrunk to less than $50. The appropriations committees generally chose to modify the authorized maximum Pell Grant, rather than to apply the reduction formula, as the means to keep program costs in line with available funds. On eight occasions, the appropriations committees devised an ad hoc formula for reducing awards in the face of limited funds. These actions by the appropriations committees nevertheless maintained the dual objectives of awarding the largest grants to students from the lowest-income families while ensuring the continued participation of students from moderate-income families.[15]

The high-water mark of the Pell Grant's reach toward students from middle-income families, reflected in MISAA, was relatively short-lived. The new Reagan administration (1981–1989) persuaded Congress to enact the Omnibus Budget Reconciliation Act of 1981, which included sharp cuts in federal student aid programs and resulted in a tilt of the Pell Grant back toward narrower targeting to students from low-income families. More recently, the reauthorization of the HEA in 1992 eliminated from consideration the asset value of the family's home in determining the expected family contribution. With this change, the pendulum once again swung the Pell Grant program somewhat more toward students from middle-income families, who are more likely to have significant home assets.

THE 1980 REAUTHORIZATION: SECTOR WARS

In 1980, the Pell Grant was extended for six years and the authorized maximum award was increased by an incremental amount for each year. The Pell Grant had become a fixture in the constellation of federal student aid programs. It was also during this reauthorization that the program was officially named for its original sponsor, Senator Pell.

One issue, however, threatened to shatter the harmony in 1980: the distribution of Pell Grants among the sectors of higher education (two-year, four-year, public, and private institutions). The associations representing the various types of institutions had only lately and reluctantly come to support the creation of the Pell Grant program in 1972. But as the Pell Grant gained acceptance and grew to levels of funding in excess of $2 billion, the associations developed an intense interest in the proportion of Pell Grant dollars that ended up in each sector of higher education.

Representative William D. Ford (D-MI), who was handling his first reauthorization of the HEA as chairman of the House Subcommittee on Postsecondary Education, was anxious to avoid a public squabble among the sectors over shares of Pell Grant dollars that could jeopardize passage of the reauthorization bill. Ford insisted that the major higher education associations negotiate an agreement among themselves on the two critical Pell Grant issues, the amount of the maximum award and the half-cost provision, which were the major factors determining the distribution of Pell Grant dollars among sectors. In turn, he promised to adopt the associations' recommendation as his own and navigate it through the legislative process with their support. The associations produced, in effect, a treaty of recommended modifications concerning the Pell Grant maximum award and the half-cost limit that was printed in the House committee report. As described in the associations' treaty, their recommendations "would build directly on the current system, proportionately expanding BEOG [Pell Grant] benefits to students attending all different types of institutions, *maintaining the balance among sectors,* and providing strong incentives for the entire community to work together in support of these expanding benefits."[16] The final legislation adopted the basic principle of the associations—significant and periodic increases in the Pell Grant maximum going hand in hand with progressive relaxation of the half-cost limitation.[17]

THE 1986 REAUTHORIZATION: LEGISLATIVE-EXECUTIVE STRUGGLES

The 1980 election, which brought Ronald Reagan to the White House, also turned control of the Senate over to the Republicans. On the Education Subcommittee, Senator Robert Stafford (R-VT) became the subcommittee chairman and Senator Pell its ranking minority member. As chairman of the subcommittee from 1981–1986, Senator Stafford continued its bipartisan tradition and orientation toward a strong federal role in support of student financial aid and equal educational opportunity, albeit with a somewhat more frugal cast.

The early 1980s were marked by an intense struggle between the legislative and executive branches over control of the Pell Grant program. As noted above, this was, in part, a disagreement about policy, with the executive branch trying to hold down costs and target Pell Grants to students from the lowest-income families while Congress was more sympathetic to including students from middle-income families. But it was also a contest for power and prerogative to determine who would control the program—another example of the struggle between the branches built into the U.S. constitutional system.

Following the passage of the Omnibus Budget Reconciliation Act of 1981, the Department of Education proposed regulations to implement the deep cuts in Pell Grant funding by increasing the percentage of discretionary income families were expected to contribute to their child's education from 10.5 percent to as much as 55 percent. This regulation would have had the effect of largely limiting Pell Grants to students from families with incomes below $15,000. These regulations were rejected by Congress through a legislative veto in December 1981. Congress also specified guidelines for the Department of Education to follow in writing new regulations for Pell Grants for the 1982-83 academic year. These guidelines resulted in significantly retrenching the Pell Grant from the broad reach into the middle class made by MISAA, although they did not narrow the program nearly as far as proposed by the Reagan administration. Through legislation adopted in 1982, 1983, and 1984, Congress required that the expected family contribution schedule and other student aid regulations in effect for the 1982-83 academic year be continued for the 1983-84 through 1986-87 academic years with updated economic assumptions. And, in 1982, Congress overrode President Reagan's veto of a supplemental appropriations bill that contained additional Pell Grant funds. In each case, a Republican-controlled Senate joined with the Democratic House to overrule the administration.

In 1983, the Supreme Court ruled in *Chadha v. Immigration and Naturalization Service* that the legislative veto was an unconstitutional intrusion by Congress into the functions of the executive branch. Thus, as Congress began the 1986 reauthorization process, it no longer had available the legislative veto to curb executive regulation of the Pell Grant. So it took the next logical step and wrote into the law the formulas for determining the expected family contribution for Pell Grants as well as other key definitions in federal student aid programs. The secretary of education's regulatory power was limited to annually updating these formulas. Congress clearly outgunned the executive branch in taking control of the levers in the Pell Grant program that determine how awards to students are calculated.

THE 1992 REAUTHORIZATION: PELL GRANT ENTITLEMENT

During the debates leading up to the enactment of the Pell Grant in 1972, many of the supporters of the new program, and none more eloquently than Senator Pell, spoke of students being "entitled" to these grants "as a matter of right." An entitlement program legally requires the government to pay benefits to all who are eligible (entitled) under the law. Spending for an entitlement program is not subject to the annual budget and appropriations process. Rather, it is governed by the number of persons eligible and the size of their benefits under the law. Unfortunately, the Pell Grant was not legislated as a legal entitlement. While the original law provided that "the Commissioner [of Education] shall . . . pay to each student . . . a basic grant" and referred to the "amount of a basic grant to which a student is entitled," the law also provided a procedure for reducing student awards in the event that "funds available for payments are insufficient to satisfy all entitlements."[18] Because the law contemplates less than automatic and full funding to meet all student "entitlements," the Pell Grant has always been treated for purposes of funding as a discretionary rather than a mandatory entitlement program.

In one limited sense, the appropriations committees have treated the Pell Grant as an entitlement. Once an appropriation act has provided an amount to fund a specified maximum grant for a given year, Congress has assumed an obligation to provide additional funding if the initial amount proves insufficient to fund the program according to the specified maximum. This goes partway toward achieving the goal of giving students early notice of the amount of grant assistance they will be guaranteed. Students do not, however, have this knowledge several years in advance to encourage them to plan their middle and high school years with higher education in mind, which would be the case if the authorized maximum Pell Grant were an entitlement.

Throughout the 1980s, and as the 1992 reauthorization approached, the Pell Grant continued to stand tall as a symbol of the federal government's commitment to equal educational opportunity for higher education through student aid. But its actual effectiveness as the engine for achieving that goal was progressively being eroded by inadequate funding. Since the 1979-80 academic year, the appropriated maximum Pell Grant has not equaled the authorized maximum. The value of the maximum award, as appropriated by Congress, declined by 40 percent in inflation-adjusted terms from the 1975-76 academic year to the 1995-96 academic year. The appropriated maximum Pell Grant as a share of average cost of attendance at private four-year colleges also declined by approximately 50 percent over the same period.[19]

As Pell Grants and other sources of grant assistance were declining in importance, their place was being taken by an increasing reliance on student loans to finance postsecondary education. This represents a shift to a weaker policy in support of equal educational opportunity, because research indicates that grants are more effective than loans in encouraging low-income students to attend college.[20] It also represents a dramatic shift in the underlying philosophy of federal student aid from its beginnings. Relying primarily on taxpayer-funded grants to attain equal educational opportunity implied that the benefits of increasing educational opportunities would be broad and public—a more socially equitable and economically productive nation. In contrast, relying primarily on loans that must be repaid with interest (self-help) to finance student participation in higher education implies that the benefits are personal and should therefore be largely borne by the individual.

The shift from grants to loans in student financial aid and the relative decline in the purchasing power of the Pell Grant led many to revive the idea of the grant as a legal entitlement—not so much as a mechanism to entice qualified low-income students into higher education but as a cure for the chronic underfunding of the program. If the Pell Grant were an entitlement, it was reasoned by the program's supporters, the appropriations would have to be sufficient to fund the authorized maximum, the total amount of grant funding would increase substantially, and the imbalance between loans and grants could be significantly improved.

In 1988, as part of a measure aimed at curbing student loan defaults, the House Education and Labor Committee approved a bill that would have made Pell Grants an entitlement. The policy rationale for including a Pell Grant entitlement in this bill was: students from low-income families have the highest student loan default rates and receive smaller Pell Grants than the maximum authorized by law. If Pell Grants were made an entitlement, students from low-income families would receive larger Pell Grants, borrow less through student loans, and default less often or, at least, on smaller loan amounts. This bill never reached the floor of the House and died at the end of the congressional session.

During the consideration of the 1992 reauthorization of the HEA, both the House Education and Labor Committee and the Senate Labor and Human Resources Committee reported bills with provisions to make Pell Grants an entitlement. The Senate committee report justified making Pell Grants an entitlement as a measure to "restore the promise it [the Pell Grant] once held in underpinning the federal government's commitment to access."[21] The House committee report noted even more starkly that "the committee believes that simply writing more authorization levels in the law will only be another exercise in making empty promises and will do nothing to redress the imbalance of loans and grants."[22] These entitlement provisions elicited fierce opposition from congressional Republicans, a veto threat from the Bush administration, muted but adamant opposition from budget-conscious Democrats (including the Democratic congressional leadership), and less than passionate support from the higher education community. As a result, the Pell Grant entitlement provisions were dropped from both the House and the Senate reauthorization bills before they reached the floor of each chamber. Without the entitlement feature, Pell Grants were reauthorized once again for six years with annual increases in the authorized maximum award but without other major changes.

PELL GRANTS, THEN AND NOW

The Pell Grant has been remarkably durable through four reauthorizations of the Higher Education Act and many other legislative enactments that have touched on the program. In fact, compared with the Pell Grant as enacted in 1972, the current program retains the same basic structure and major provisions. Today's Pell Grant is still:

- a portable voucher that students can use to pay for postsecondary education at a broad range of eligible institutions, including almost all the more than 3,000 two- and four-year nonprofit colleges and universities as well as several thousand for-profit institutions, most of which offer short-term occupational training programs.

- a need-based grant that targets most of its benefits to students from low-income families while making some aid available to students from moderate- and middle-income families.

- a grant expressed in terms of a fixed maximum award. The intent of this feature was to inform students of the size of the award they could anticipate some years in advance of their actual enrollment in postsecondary education. However, the effectiveness of this feature has been significantly diminished by funding shortfalls. The appropriated maximum has not equaled the authorized maximum since the 1979-80 academic year. Thus a student only knows the maximum established by appropriation one year in advance.

- a grant in which the actual award is calculated by subtracting a measure of the student's family's ability to pay from the maximum award.

- a grant that complements existing campus-based programs (Supplemental Educational Opportunity Grants, College Work-Study, and National Defense/Direct/Perkins Loans) rather than replaces them. The trigger or threshold provision in the Pell Grant program, which was intended to ensure through legislation continued funding for campus-based programs, was repealed in the 1986 reauthorization because it was unnecessary, but the policy of maintaining both Pell Grants and campus-based programs as elements of the federal student aid system has clearly not been abandoned.

There are three major differences between the Pell Grant program of today and the program as initially enacted. First, the cost-of-education allowance that was a feature of both Senator Pell's original 1969 bill and the Pell Grant as enacted in 1972 was never funded and therefore never implemented. It was repealed in 1992 with little notice or regret. The 1972 legislation provided that these allowances would be based largely on the number of federally aided students attending an institution and the amount of federal student aid they received. In theory, the idea was that students receiving federal student aid were likely to need some extra support from institutions and that these allowances would defray those additional costs. The allowances would therefore encourage institutions to recruit, admit, and retain such students, thereby contributing to broader educational opportunity. In fact, however, the cost-of-attendance allowances were a sop from the victorious student-aid advocates to the defeated supporters of institutional aid in 1972. Because the allowances scarcely resembled the capitation grants supported by the institutional-aid advocates and because the student-aid advocates had little use for them beyond their political function, there was never any strong support for funding or implementing them, and they were a dead letter.

Second, the 1972 act provided that the schedule of expected family contributions (the measure of student and family ability to pay) would be established by regulations promulgated by the administration but subject to a legislative veto by Congress. Following the Supreme Court's 1983 decision declaring the legislative veto unconstitutional, and several years of tense policy disagreements with the administration over who should benefit from Pell Grants, Congress seized the power to determine financial need by writing the methodology for determining expected family contribution into law. This was arguably an extension of the original intent of the 1972 act, which had provided for legislative veto of the administration's proposed family contribution regulations and had specified in the law the basic criteria to be followed in promulgating these regulations.

Third, the half-cost provision was repealed in 1992. This provision was intended to introduce a measure of choice into the Pell Grant program in addition to promoting access. The idea was that if students could not use their Pell Grants to pay the entire charge of a low-cost institution, they would consider a broader range of choices, including high-priced institutions. Policymakers were ultimately persuaded, however, that the unfairness of cutting the grants of students from the lowest-income families could not be justified by the hypothetical benefit of promoting greater choice. Choice may still remain a goal of federal student aid policy as a whole, but the Pell Grant focuses almost exclusively on access.

In one other important respect, the Pell Grant program of today probably does not look like the program that existed in the mind's eye of its creators in 1972. And that is in the profile of the recipients. It is always risky to try to read the minds of politicians, particularly after a quarter century has elapsed. Nevertheless, I believe most of the Pell Grant supporters in Congress in 1972 envisioned the "traditional" student as the principal beneficiary of the program: the 18-to-24-year-old who is in full-time attendance at a four-year, baccalaureate-granting institution that the student entered directly after high school and who relies on his or her parents to pay a major share of postsecondary educational costs. As we all know, the "nontraditional" student, who is older, attending part-time, attending a non-baccalaureate-granting institution, and independent of parental support, has at least achieved parity in numbers with the traditional student in postsecondary education. Indeed, independent students now represent almost 60 percent of all Pell Grant recipients.[23] The Pell Grant as enacted in 1972 explicitly included independent students and those attending less than full time. However, the Pell Grant program of today probably has more older students and fewer full-time and dependent students than its sponsors envisioned. It certainly would have sounded a discordant note in 1972 to talk of large numbers of Pell Grant recipients in "job training" rather than "academic" or "college" programs.

FINAL THOUGHTS

Outside the circle of those directly involved in its creation, the enactment of the Pell Grant was scarcely remarked upon at the time President Nixon signed the omnibus education bill of which it was a part in June 1972. The creation of the Pell Grant was overshadowed by the controversy surrounding school busing amendments. However, one of the most active participants in the legislative struggle to enact the Pell Grant program, Congressman Al Quie (R-MN), looked over the horizon and made a prediction. "I believe the basic educational opportunity [Pell] grant will be looked upon in years ahead as one of the great achievements in federal higher education legislation," he said.[24] He was prescient, because the program has endured for a quarter of a century and become one of the centerpieces of federal higher education policy.

There is a paradox to the Pell Grant program. It was born in controversy and it has always been surrounded by controversy, yet it has never had serious opposition. There has never been a significant effort to terminate or repeal the program, even when sentiment for shrinking the federal government's domestic programs was at its peak in President Reagan's first term and after the Republican takeover of Congress following the 1994 election. The broad support for and longevity of the program reflect the solidity of its foundation. The ideal of equal educational opportunity in higher education remains a powerful political symbol in the United States, and the Pell Grant stands as the embodiment of the federal government's commitment to this ideal. The challenge for the future is how to restore the Pell Grant as the real foundation, and not just the symbol, of equal educational opportunity.

THOMAS R. WOLANIN *is a research professor of educational policy and political science at George Washington University. He is also a senior associate at The Institute for Higher Education Policy, focusing on issues of postsecondary finance, student access, and federal policy development. He was previously deputy assistant secretary for legislation in the U.S. Department of Education, and before that staff director of the Subcommittee on Postsecondary Education in the U.S. House of Representatives. Wolanin received his B.A. from Oberlin College and a Ph.D. from Harvard University.*

NOTES

1. Senator Edward M. Kennedy (D-MA), *Congressional Record,* May 24, 1972, 18858.
2. These broad national benefits are labeled positive externalities by economists.
3. John F. Morse, "How We Got Here from There—A Personal Reminiscence of the Early Days," in *Student Loans: Problems and Policy,* ed. Lois D. Rice (New York: College Entrance Examination Board, 1977), 3–4.
4. "Special Message to the Congress: Toward Full Educational Opportunity," January 12, 1965, *Public Papers of the Presidents,* 30.
5. "Remarks at Southwest Texas State College Upon Signing the Higher Education Act of 1965," November 8, 1965, *Public Papers of the Presidents,* 1102.
6. "Special Message to the Congress on Higher Education," March 19, 1970, *Public Papers of the Presidents,* 276 and 278.

7. "Special Message to the Congress on Higher Education," February 22, 1971, *Public Papers of the Presidents,* 196. On the development of the Nixon administration's higher education proposal, see Lawrence E. Gladieux and Thomas R. Wolanin, *Congress and the Colleges: The National Politics of Higher Education* (Lexington, MA: D.C. Heath, 1976), 57–81. The Nixon administration proposal is conceptually quite similar to the Student's Total Education Package (STEP) proposal recommended by the National Commission on Responsibilities for Financing Postsecondary Education in its *Final Report: Making College Affordable* (Washington, D.C., 1993).

8. On the ferment of policy thinking and proposals leading up to the adoption of Pell Grants, see Gladieux and Wolanin, *Congress and the Colleges,* 35–56.

9. *Congressional Record,* April 25, 1969, 10434-35.

10. Gladieux and Wolanin, *Congress and the Colleges,* 98.

11. "Special Message to the Congress on Higher Education," March 19, 1970, *Public Papers of the Presidents,* 278.

12. See, for example, statement of Senator Pell, *Congressional Record,* April 25, 1969, 10435, and statement by Congressman John Brademas, *Congressional Record,* June 8, 1972, 20293.

13. On the 1976 reauthorization and the private colleges, see Lawrence E. Gladieux and Thomas R. Wolanin, "Federal Politics," in *Public Policy and Private Higher Education,* eds. David W. Breneman and Chester E. Finn, (Washington, D.C.: The Brookings Institution, 1978).

14. *Congressional Record,* April 25, 1969, 10435.

15. Because the reduction formula was being routinely superseded in the appropriations process, in the 1992 reauthorization the authorizing committees basically surrendered to the appropriations committees the power to adjust Pell Grant awards in relation to available funds and repealed the reduction formula. See "Higher Education Amendments of 1992," Conference Report to accompany S.1150, House Report No. 102-630, 429–30.

16. "Education Amendments of 1980," House of Representatives Report No. 96-520, 18 (emphasis added).

17. In the reauthorizations of 1986 and 1992, the major higher education associations continued to produce consensus Pell Grant recommendations. The House Education and Labor Committee and the Senate Labor and Human Resources Committee generally followed their lead on the issues of the Pell Grant maximum and the half-cost provision. The potentially divisive issue of sector shares was left to be passionately debated in the inner sanctums of One Dupont Circle. These debates were largely academic, however, because the actual appropriated maximum Pell Grant did not equal the authorized maximum after the 1979-80 academic year.

18. PL 92-318, Section 411(a)(1), Section 411(a)(2)(B)(i), and Section 411(b)(3)(B)(i).

19. College Board, *Trends in Student Aid: 1987 to 1997* (New York: College Entrance Examination Board, 1997), Table 7 and Figure 6, 13.

20. See, for example, U.S. General Accounting Office, *Restructuring Student Aid Could Reduce Low-Income Student Dropout Rate* (Washington, D.C.: U.S. General

Accounting Office, 1995) and Edward St. John, "The Impact of Student Financial Aid: A Review of Recent Research," *Journal of Student Financial Aid* 24: 1 (1994), 5-12.

21. "Reauthorizing the Higher Education Act of 1965," Senate Report No. 102-204, 23.

22. "Higher Education Amendments of 1992," House Report No. 102-447, 25.

23. College Board, *Trends in Student Aid: 1987 to 1997*, Table 7.

24. *Congressional Record*, June 8, 1972, 20286.

Linking Access and Aspirations: The Dual Purpose of Pell Grants

Martin A. Kramer

Abstract. *The original Pell Grant program was about more than financial aid. Its framers incorporated specific features that they hoped would spark the motivation of students early in their schooling to consider college as a realistic possibility and prepare academically. Such motivational considerations were part of the reason for not having a competitive merit selection process that might discourage students lacking self-confidence. Students needed only to complete high school to be eligible, a goal more easily envisioned (and worked for) than admission to a selective institution. The same idea of making college aspirations achievable was also a reason for making the amount of the award predictable. That purpose should now be reinforced by making the Pell Grant maximum an amount adequate to meet minimum higher education expenses and the award amount certain and easy to calculate while students are still in high school and making their plans for after graduation.*

To many of those who now benefit from the program and to many of those involved in one way or another in its administration, the Pell Grant must look like a rather mechanical distribution of money to eligible students and a denial of funding to others. Because the real value of the grants has been shrunk by inflation and diluted by an expanded population of eligible students, it must now be a rare case in which a Pell Grant is seen as critical in purchasing educational opportunity—that is, as making a decisive difference in whether a student goes to college or not.

LEARNING FROM HISTORY

In thinking about the future of Pell Grants, it is worth going beyond a purely mechanical view of the program. In doing this, we would do well to think again about the assumptions of the program at the time it was enacted. How did people expect the mechanisms of the program to work? Why were these regarded as the right mechanisms? To what policy purposes? How was the program expected to engage the aspirations of the students who were to benefit from it? Whether the assumptions of the program on these points were (or were not) valid at the time, we need to ask whether they are valid now. Are the hopes buried in these assumptions still our hopes? If so, what still needs to be done to realize them?

A short answer to these questions would go something like this: Many people (most clearly, many young people) who could benefit from some form of postsecondary education were not receiving that opportunity in the 1960s because they could not afford the cost, even the cost of subsistence at institutions at which tuition was free. The difference between them and their more fortunate contemporaries was primarily a difference in the amount of money their parents could contribute to their educational expenses. Accordingly, a program was needed that would neutralize such differences and thereby reduce intergenerational inequality in access to higher education. Means test mechanisms for such a program had been demonstrated to be administratively feasible. Further, these mechanisms permitted cost estimates that would make such a program affordable as a federal budget priority. A program that employed these mechanisms could mesh effectively with other federal efforts to expand educational opportunities beyond high school, such as the National Defense Student Loan, the Educational Opportunity Grant, and the College Work-Study programs, and it would give potential students the kind of realistic hope for their future that would engage them in preparing and planning for college.

THE BRAVE NEW WORLD OF 1972

A more adequate response to the questions posed previously requires, however, that we look more closely at the historical context of the Pell Grant program. U.S. egalitarianism has deep roots, but some concepts incorporated in the program were of much more recent origin. Ideas of social utility and social mobility through education have a very long history in the United States, but it is hard to imagine a program like the Pell Grant having been enacted and funded in an earlier period. A generation earlier, many people would have said that universal access to higher education was a wonderful ideal but a highly impractical one. In the world of 1972, new circumstances made it seem an entirely practical goal.

One of the circumstances new in the 1970s was the widening availability of public community colleges and the prospect that they would
soon be accessible to almost all Americans. Some states had gone much
further than others in siting community colleges within commuting reach
of their citizens, but laggard states were catching up. In this period, new
community colleges were opening around the nation at the rate of about
one per week.

The growth of public community colleges was on a separate legislative and administrative track from concurrent developments in student
financial aid, but that separation should not conceal the enormous impact
the availability of community colleges had on federal aid policy.
Community colleges were in the process of pulling down roughly half
of the barrier to universal access to higher education, the half represented
by tuition and housing costs. These institutions charged low or zero
tuition, and their geographic accessibility to commuters minimized out-
of-pocket outlays for subsistence costs. Subsistence continued to be a
barrier to access, but it had, in effect, been pared down to a point at which
the financing of a national program to get students over this final obstacle began to seem a manageable budget priority.

Further, meaningful access could now be offered to the general run
of students—not like, for example, the highly selective access that poor
but exceptionally brilliant students already had to Ivy League colleges.
The new community colleges were not elitist, did not demand outstanding
academic performance, and offered a broad spectrum of academic and
occupational training programs. They were conceptually, and usually
administratively, an extension of the accepted concepts of free elementary and secondary education and the values of universal literacy.

A second element of the context in which the Pell Grant program was
conceived was the nation's experience with the GI Bill after World War II
(also a personal experience for many people in policy positions by the
1970s). The early GI Bill had dealt effectively with both the financial
barrier to access posed by tuition charges and the barrier of subsistence
costs. Its effects had been dramatic for students, institutions, and the
national economy. We speak today of "nontraditional students," but
many GI Bill students were nontraditional in a much more radical sense:
They were often not only the first in their families to attend college but
the first from their neighborhoods to take advantage of an opportunity never realistically available before. The practical success of the GI
Bill in creating such opportunities was frequently cited by proponents

of the Pell Grant idea. In the rhetoric of the time, it would be a "universal GI Bill."

A third factor coloring the thinking behind the Pell Grant program was the War on Poverty of the preceding decade. There was ample evidence that poverty was often transmitted from generation to generation, despite a growing economy, free public education (through high school anyway), and a variety of public supports for impoverished families. The War on Poverty took as one of its premises the desirability of additional interventions specifically designed to equalize life chances and thereby "break the cycle of poverty." Student financial aid seemed a promising kind of specific intervention, because it would give students the financial help their families could not provide to take an educational route out of poverty. College Work-Study, Upward Bound, and student grants were accordingly created and funded by the Office of Economic Opportunity.

The assumption that student financial aid could be highly effective in promoting social mobility was not simply hopeful rhetoric or based on mere anecdotes. There was respectable social science evidence that young people with the academic ability to attend college were much more likely to enroll if they came from affluent families rather than from poor ones. This suggested to many that differences in financial resources explained differences in rates of attendance. If so, efforts to equalize financial resources for college would tend to equalize attendance rates and thereby life chances. To be sure, there might be differences in preparation, motivation, culture, and the availability of noncollege opportunities that accounted for some of the differences in enrollment rates, but these too seemed amenable to intervention, as demonstrated by the Upward Bound program.

Important also were precedents for the administrative feasibility of a program like the Pell Grant. Equalizing the financial resources available for college might well have seemed administratively too difficult for practical policy a generation before. But by the 1970s, there were precedents that made such a policy appear highly "doable." One was the development of a need analysis system by the College Board's College Scholarship Service. The existence of this system and its adoption by many colleges and several state aid programs provided assurance that a reasonably good measure of the differences in the ability of families to pay for college could be developed. The system had also been adopted, first by the National Defense Student Loan program and then by aid programs transferred from the Office of Economic Opportunity to the U.S. Office of Education. Thus a federal precedent was established for using a need analysis system to measure the widely different capacities of families to pay for the cost of higher education.

APPLYING THE LESSONS

This historical background explains important features of the Pell Grant program. The College Scholarship Service precedent made it reasonable to design the program around a uniform, national need analysis system. The resulting "expected family contribution" could be deducted from a modest estimate of the costs of attending a postsecondary institution, with the program awarding a grant equal to the difference. It could be a modest estimate because the costs of attending a low- or zero-tuition community college (mainly subsistence costs) could be established as the amount of the maximum Pell Grant.

Both the differences and the similarities between the Pell Grant program and the post-World War II GI Bill played a part in the structure adopted for the Pell Grant. The GI Bill had no means test, while under the new program students from middle- and upper-income families would be eligible only for small grants, or no grants, because of the need analysis system. This meant that the aggregate cost of grants under the new program would be much more manageable from a budgetary point of view than a true universal GI Bill. A second difference was that only trivial tuition and fee charges need be recognized in estimating total per-student costs of attendance (and the Pell Grant maximum) if, as pointed out before, the costs of attending a public community college were the standard, rather than those of the private, four-year colleges or state universities many GI Bill students had attended. Precisely because the Pell Grant program would not be like the GI Bill in these respects, a universal GI Bill would not be too expensive.

Yet the Pell Grant program would be similar to the GI Bill in some respects. The student would have a choice of college and, provided the college admitted the student, no assessment of academic ability would be a prerequisite for eligibility. Further, subsistence costs would be recognized and at least partially removed as a barrier to access, as under the GI Bill. It thus seemed reasonable to hope that the program would have similar dramatic effects on social mobility.

We can think of the Pell Grant program as following a policy recipe: Combine one part adoption of low estimates of per-student costs (from the community college experience), one part recognition of subsistence costs as the main remaining barrier to access (from the GI Bill and the community college experience), and one part a means test of proved feasibility (from the College Scholarship Service experience). Mix well, and the nation could afford a modest but universal guarantee of resources for college, without restrictive academic eligibility rules and with choice of college.

THE MOTIVATIONAL ASSUMPTIONS

But one more ingredient was needed to give the recipe its full flavor: a view of the motivation of low-income students was at the foundation of the Pell Grant program. Some people assumed, of course, that if money for college was provided, this was enough. But others thought it was also important to consider how a new grant program would engage the aspirations of students hitherto lacking access to college.

Those addressing this question of engagement tended to base their thinking on a particular analysis of student motivation. Their concern was that going to college would be a daunting prospect for many of the students the Pell Grant would target by its family income test. Many of these students had had bad experiences with K-12 education and lacked the confidence in themselves that would enable them to see the opportunity to attend college as readily within their grasp, in the way that upper-middle-income students did. Accordingly, low-income students needed to feel certain enough that college was a realistic option—realistic because they would have enough money to pay for it—so that they would begin thinking of themselves as future college students and do the groundwork to plan and prepare themselves.

Most of the rest of this paper is devoted to the implications of this motivational premise, to the question of whether it was right or wrong then—and whether it is now. If it is right, I suggest that increasing the size of the Pell Grant maximum is the most important initiative that could be taken to improve the present system.

The motivational rationale does explain a good deal about why there was real enthusiasm for certain features of the Pell Grant program. The grants were designed to be portable, not just because of the GI Bill precedent or just to support market forces (as is often emphasized) but also to assure students that they would not have to go through a particular institution's intimidating and competitive admission process to receive financial aid. No grade-point or test score requirements were imposed for the same reason—to avoid creating an additional hurdle for students lacking confidence in their academic ability.

Further, the deduction of an assessed expected family contribution from the legislated maximum grant was intended to yield a firm dollar figure for the amount of grant eligibility, although it has not done so in fact. This figure would enable students and their parents to calculate how much additional money it would take to attend any college of given cost, if not a local community college. The idea was that the Pell Grant would make it worthwhile to start planning for college. This advance assurance of support would also give high school teachers and counselors something they could work with to raise student aspirations. Their urgings could not easily be dismissed as mere feel-good optimism: cash would actually be on the table.

It may help here to contrast Pell Grants with the National Merit Scholarship program. That excellent program also has a motivational rationale—to encourage young people already launched on a successful educational career to try to do even better. But it is a different rationale, with a very different kind of leverage on student aspirations, than the Pell Grant.

THE EVIDENCE

Were these 1972 ideas about the motivating role of student aid valid? One, but only one, of the assumptions involved can be easily validated. The evidence is right there in the National Longitudinal Study and High School and Beyond data: If you plan for college, you are much more likely actually to go. High school students who take the SAT®, or who take college preparatory courses, or who are told—by just about any significant person in their lives—that they should think about college are much more likely in fact to go than other students of similar ability and family income who have not planned for college in these ways.

Beyond this evidence, although the motivational assumptions behind the Pell Grant concept made a certain amount of intuitive sense, they also represented a considerable leap into the psychological dark. They did reflect the experience of some programs, such as Upward Bound, that making going to college a more practical possibility seemed to stimulate motivation, but these were originally small programs characterized by careful selection of participants.

Given that the motivational assumptions of the Pell Grant were not on very secure ground when it was enacted, did experience bear them out? As early as the late 1970s, the results of the program disappointed some people, especially those who had been carried away in their enthusiasm for a universal GI Bill. Some dashing of these hopes was inevitable, because, as we have seen, the Pell Grant was not identical to the GI Bill.

Yet there were substantial increases in college-going rates for both low-income men and women in the three or four years immediately after 1972. In this period, the constant-dollar value of the Pell Grant was at its maximum, as was the value of grants under some large state programs. And, in the same period, other powerful motivational factors were at work: Colleges were making major, if sometimes chaotic, efforts to recruit low-income, especially minority, students. Recruiters were assuring low-income students that they could make a success of college. Thus, the Pell Grant was implemented at a time when it could reinforce, and be reinforced by, other motivational factors.

My conclusion is that the early experience of the Pell Grant—not the more recent experience—may plausibly, if not compellingly, validate the motivational assumptions underlying the program. It is then also plausible to suggest that a large increase in the maximum Pell Grant could make the program work better, possibly much better, because the maximum grant needs to be large enough to engage the aspirations of students in the way originally intended. It is hard to find any reason why making college aspirations genuinely realizable should not be just as important now as it was in 1972 in engaging the efforts of low-income students to achieve better futures for themselves.

Those who think that it is not desirable, practical, or of the highest priority to provide sufficient financial aid to low-income students so that they can attend college are turning their backs, however reluctantly, on a central rationale of the present Pell Grant system. A strongly merit-oriented system, for example, would effectively say, "We don't think the aid system can be expected to supply critical motivational support to students who lack self-confidence." That proposition should be explicitly examined before it is implicitly accepted.

CERTAINTY OF ELIGIBILITY

The universality of access promised by the Pell Grant was, of course, part of its grand vision, but universal eligibility also would have a highly practical consequence. Because all students could receive aid if they met the program's family-income criteria, then aid could be counted upon. The certainty of receiving aid was almost as important as the adequacy of the Pell maximum to meet minimum educational costs. For an offer of opportunity to low-income students to be credible, the argument went, it must also be a firm offer. For the offer to form a basis for future plans, it must be made before it is too late, that is, early in the student's high school career. That, in turn, means a funding commitment from the political powers-that-be years in advance of the actual award of aid to a particular student. It just is not good enough for a high school guidance counselor to say to a student, "You seem smart enough to go to college. If we are not in a recession when you graduate, if there isn't another convulsion of guilt about deficits, if there isn't another taxpayer revolt, you can expect adequate aid."

Does this mean that federal student financial aid must become another dreaded entitlement? Not necessarily. It is, after all, quite possible for Congress to advance fund programs four or five years into the future. No entitlement is created in that case. It is also possible to build a consensus that certain programs should have "sacred cow" status. A good many programs have such status, whether they are technically entitlements or not. Why not student aid?

But making a long-term commitment to student aid should not be made to sound too easy by pointing out that such aid does not technically have to be an entitlement. It is important to make clear that, for the Pell Grant system to have much hope of working as intended, it must represent something very much like an entitlement in practice. One of the basic premises of the program put together in 1972 was advance assurance of support. The Pell Grant was intended to motivate millions of students performing below their potential. It was thought that this could not be done with an "iffy" or highly conditional offer of aid.

This rationale, and not a disregard of academic values, was one of the reasons there were to be no merit criteria for the Pell Grants. Introducing merit criteria of more than the most modest sort would be inconsistent with the original rationale, even in an effort to concentrate funds and give larger awards to fewer students. We must face the fact that, if we do not think federal student grants should be something very close to an entitlement, then we really should go back to the drawing boards. By all means, consolidate programs, reduce dilution, and target grants at students for whom they will really make a difference in order to increase the size of the maximum grant. The adequacy of the Pell Grant maximum for meeting minimum educational costs is crucial. But so is advance assurance of support.

MARTIN A. KRAMER *is a policy analyst and commentator on higher education. Formerly a senior fellow at the Carnegie Council on Policy Studies in Higher Education, he is editor-in-chief of* New Directions in Higher Education, *and a contributing author to* Change *magazine. From 1969 to 1977, Kramer was director of higher education planning and then acting assistant secretary for education planning in the Department of Health, Education, and Welfare, where he helped shape the Basic Grant program. He received his B.A. from Harvard University and his D.Phil. as a Rhodes Scholar from Trinity College at Oxford University.*

1972: SCENES FROM THE HOUSE/SENATE CONFERENCE COMMITTEE THAT ESTABLISHED THE PELL GRANT PROGRAM

Left to right, Senators Robert Stafford (R-VT), Peter Dominick (R-CO), and Claiborne Pell (D-RI), chairman of the Senate education subcommittee, meeting with their House colleagues on the 1972 reauthorization of the Higher Education Act.

Rep. Carl Perkins (D-KY), left, chair of the House Committee on Education and Labor, and Rep. Albert Quie (R-MN), ranking Republican member of the subcommittee on higher education.

Representative Edith Green (D-OR), right, chair of the House subcommittee on higher education, and staff aide Sally Kirkgasler, now with the U.S. Department of Education.

Rep. Perkins, right, and Rep. Roman Pucinski (D-IL), who chaired the House subcommittee on elementary and secondary education.

The conference committee met for two difficult months to resolve the 400 differences between the House and Senate bills: left to right, former staff aide Tom Wolanin; Reps. John Brademas (D-IN), Pucinski, Frank Thompson (D-NJ), and Green; staff counsel Bill Gaul; and Chairman Perkins.

Rep. Pucinski (right) with staff counsel Jack Jennings and Rep. Brademas.

Three pivotal Republican members of the conference committee, left to right, Reps. John Erlenborn (R-IL), John Dellenback (R-OR), and William Steiger (R-WI).

Rep. Dellenback, center, with Senators Dominick and Pell. Senator Pell's tenacity ensured that the Basic Educational Opportunity Grant was in the final agreement.

© Marty LaVor

© Marty LaVor

Senator Jacob Javits (R-NY), a liberal Republican and key mediating influence in the conference committee.

© Marty LaVor

A late-night informal caucus: Senators Edward Kennedy (D-MA), Alan Cranston (D-CA), and Tom Eagleton (D-MO).

Eleventh-hour politics in the Capitol.

© Marty LaVor

At the negotiating table, left to right: Senators Dominick and Pell; staff aide Richard Smith; Senators Kennedy, Walter Mondale (D-MN), and Cranston; unidentified; and Rep. William Lehman (D-FL).

Left to right (seated), Senators Kennedy and Mondale, with (standing) Reps. Pucinski and Perkins and Senator Pell. The political skills of Senator Pell and Rep. Perkins were critical to forging a compromise.

The House/Senate conference committee reached final agreement at 5:13 a.m. on May 17, 1972, ensuring passage of the bill that would establish the Basic Educational Opportunity Grant (later renamed the Pell Grant).

Left to right, Reps. Brademas, Quie, and Perkins and Senators Pell and Dominick present the conference agreement to the press.

Reason

The idea of the "basic grant" was simple: a foundation of support for needy students to attend college. Its implementation and impact were and are more complicated.

Evidence of the program's effectiveness is necessarily suggestive rather than clearcut. It is difficult to separate out the influence of Pell Grants from related student aid policies as well as as other factors that determine enrollment and success in higher education. But there are important indicators to consider.

In "Reason," our authors pour over a quarter century of experience and trend data to gauge the intended and unintended outcomes of the Pell Grant program. These analyses provide us with some answers, a few surprises, and more questions. Ultimately they help us better understand the complexities of the Pell Grant program.

The Vision and Reality
of Pell Grants:
Unforeseen Consequences
for Students and Institutions

Sarah E. Turner

Abstract. *Outcomes of the Pell Grant program have not been confined to a reduction in college costs for low-income, traditional-age college students. The availability of Pell Grant dollars has allowed some institutions to invest more of their own resources in students who are above the Pell Grant eligibility range but still of moderate financial means. Moreover, older, independent students may have experienced the largest declines in net college costs as well as the largest increases in enrollment as a result of Pell Grants. Indirect, largely unintended effects also include the proliferation of proprietary schools, many of which might not have been economically viable without the introduction of substantial federal student aid, and increases in the numbers of midcareer workers seeking retraining in the postsecondary system. In shaping Pell Grants for the twenty-first century and allocating scarce resources, policymakers should ask whether the one-size-fits-all funding approach—for collegiate and noncollegiate postsecondary training, for rehabilitative investment in older workers, and for preparation of young workers—leads to the best outcomes for individuals and society.*

In recent years, policymakers and researchers interested in whether means-tested financial aid is a potent policy instrument to increase college participation among low-income students have looked at the experience of the Pell Grant program for guidance. Despite high hopes from its founders and strong encouragement from early research, the enrollment gap between the most economically disadvantaged students and students from other income groups does not appear to have narrowed. In fact, the gap may have widened over the past 25 years.

In one of the first assessments of the Pell Grant program, Lee Hansen compared college enrollment levels of more- and less-affluent students before and after the introduction of the program. He concluded that "the expansion of federal financial aid programs and their targeting toward youth from lower-income and lower-status families did not alter to any appreciable degree the composition of postsecondary students or the college enrollment expectations of high school seniors over the 1970s."[1] These findings did not accord with the popularly-held expectation that the growth in the availability of financial aid to low-income youth would lead to substantial increases in college participation.

Such assessments of the effectiveness of the Pell Grant program that focus on the behavior of traditional college-aged students are almost certain to be too narrow. If there is a general lesson to be learned from the quarter century of the Pell Grant program, it is that higher education is not a static system and, therefore, it is very difficult to target financial aid. The effects of programs like Pell Grants are highly likely to spill over to other income groups, primarily because educational institutions will alter their policies in response to any federal initiative. In this sense, higher education in the United States is a dynamic market that responds, perhaps more rapidly than some skeptics would acknowledge, to changes in incentives and shifts in student demand.

The first part of this paper describes the basic parameters and initial goals of the Pell Grant program and the evolution of federal support for higher education over the last three decades. The next part discusses some of the responses to the introduction of the Pell Grant made by postsecondary institutions. In particular, three adjustments in the postsecondary marketplace appear to have been facilitated by the Pell Grant program:

1. Reductions in net college costs for students of moderate financial means, in addition to some decline in college costs for very low-income students. The allocation of financial aid by institutions of higher education "undid" some of the income-targeting efforts of the Pell Grant program.

2. Dramatic increases in college enrollment among older students because financing mechanisms (including loan programs as well as the Pell Grant) made postsecondary education financially viable and institutions adjusted their offerings to meet the needs of these students.

3. A rapid increase in the number of proprietary (for-profit) postsecondary institutions in response to the new subsidy for higher education implicit in the Pell program.

The final section considers the future of federal financial aid, with particular emphasis on the Pell Grant program. The challenge for policymakers is to think broadly about how the market for higher education is likely to adapt to changes in the availability of federal financial aid and whether the full range of outcomes is consistent with the legislative objective.

THE FEDERAL COMMITMENT TO FINANCIAL AID FOR HIGHER EDUCATION

From the beginning, the objective of the Pell Grant program has been to provide a base grant to students from low-income backgrounds to reduce the cost of college attendance. The Pell Grant was distinguished from other need-based programs in that awards were portable grants to individual students, although the amount of the awards depended to some extent on college costs. The anticipated behavioral outcome was that the price of college would be reduced by the Pell Grant amount for eligible students and that this reduction would encourage economically disadvantaged individuals to enroll in college.

Eligibility for both Pell Grants and more general means-tested financial aid is based on a tax rate on assets and income less an adjustment for family size and other costs of living. The expected family contribution to college costs is the sum of the student's contribution (reflecting a combination of savings and earnings) and the parents' contribution. In essence, this latter amount is the product of the computed adjusted available income and a contribution rate. The Pell Grant award is the maximum grant amount in any given year minus the computed expected family contribution.

The basic logic of award calculation has remained constant since the program's inception, but parameters such as the assessment rates applied to assets and income and the adjustments for family size have varied over time. In addition, program variables such as the maximum and minimum Pell Grant amounts are set in nominal terms, with the result that year-to-year changes in award levels often fail to keep pace with inflation. Figure 1 illustrates the variation in the real value of the maximum Pell award over the past 25 years.

Table 1 shows an overall increase in the federal government's role in financing higher education between 1970 and 1980 following the introduction of the Pell Grant program in 1972. The Pell Grant underscored the commitment of the federal government to providing a floor of portable financial aid, distributed entirely on the basis of need. The program grew quickly, and by 1980-81 accounted for nearly one-third of all federal grants to students. The aggregates reported in Table 1 provide a broad measure of how the total pool of resources for subsidizing higher education changed; equally important, but not shown in the table, is the changing distribution of these resources among students from different economic levels. While the total level of student financial aid grew over this interval, the range of students receiving support expanded to include more older, nontraditional students. Although these aggregate figures are suggestive, the extent to which these forces coalesced to affect the college costs of individual students from different economic and educational backgrounds remains unclear from the data.

The real value of aid from institutional sources—the direct resources provided by colleges and universities—remained nearly constant dur-

FIGURE 1.   *Trends in Authorized and Actual Maximum Pell Grant Award (in constant 1994 U.S. dollars)*

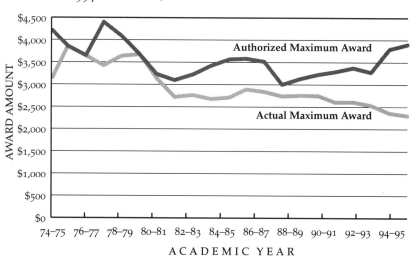

Source: College Board, *Trends in Student Aid: 1998.*

TABLE 1.   *Aid Awarded to Students by Source of Aid (in millions of 1994 U.S. dollars)*

	1970-71		1980-81		1990-91		1994-95	
	$	*% of Aid*	$	*% of Aid*	$	*% of Aid*	$	*% of Aid*
Federal Programs								
Generally Available Aid								
Pell Grants	0	0.0%	4,088	14.2%	5,436	17.0%	5,570	12.1%
SEOG	499	3.0%	630	2.2%	501	1.6%	546	1.2%
SSIG	0	0.0%	124	0.4%	65	0.2%	72	0.2%
Work-Study	849	5.1%	1,131	3.9%	806	2.5%	749	1.6%
Perkins Loans	898	5.4%	1,188	4.1%	964	3.0%	958	2.1%
GSL, PLUS, and SLS	3,791	22.9%	10,623	37.0%	14,034	44.0%	24,325	52.7%
Specially Directed Aid								
Social Security	1,864	11.3%	3,225	11.2%	0	0.0%	0	0.0%
Veterans	4,187	25.3%	2,936	10.2%	752	2.4%	1,390	3.0%
Other	457	2.8%	659	2.3%	920	2.9%	999	2.2%
Total Federal Aid	12,545	75.8%	24,604	85.6%	23,478	73.6%	34,610	75.0%
State Grant Programs	882	5.3%	1,372	4.8%	2,059	6.5%	2,628	5.7%
Institutionally Awarded Aid	3,125	18.9%	2,782	9.7%	6,379	20.0%	8,929	19.3%
Total	16,552	100.0%	28,758	100.0%	31,916	100.0%	46,167	100.0%

Source: McPherson, Michael and Morton Owen Schapiro, *The Student Aid Game: Meeting Need and Rewarding Talent in American Higher Education* (Princeton, N.J.: Princeton University Press, 1996), Table 3.3.
Notes: GSL: Guaranteed Student Loans, PLUS: Parent Loans for Undergraduate Students, SLS: Supplemental Loans for Students, SEOG: Supplemental Educational Opportunity Grant, and SSIG: State Student Incentive Grant. Totals may not be exact due to rounding.

ing the 1970s and then increased markedly during the 1980s. Although the total share of financial aid from institutional sources decreased from nearly 20 percent in the 1970-71 academic year to about 10 percent in 1980-81 before rising again to about 20 percent in 1990-91, this trend disguises sizable shifts in the distribution of enrollment between different types of institutions. Ideally, we would like to be able to measure the change in the allocation of institutional resources per student at a range of different types of colleges and universities.

Table 1 also shows the shift in federal financing of higher education from grants to loans in the 1980s. Not only do federal loan programs partially resolve the absence of a private credit market for higher education costs, but they also encompass elements of subsidy through deferred interest payments, federal guarantee of principal, and below-market interest rates. The extent to which the infusion of loan funds represents a net increase in federal financial aid rests critically on the subsidy value, and that value depends on the duration of a student's education. Most economists estimate this value to be no more than 50 percent, though the estimate varies depending on the student's educational trajectory and the particular federal program for which the student is eligible.[2] As a practical matter, however, it is difficult to assign a value to these subsidies before the duration of college enrollment is known because the subsidies are more valuable if the student enrolls in college for a longer period of time.

The eligibility threshold in federally subsidized loan programs has historically been considerably higher than in the Pell Grant program. Thus the shift in emphasis to loans at the federal level in the early 1980s represented a change in the distribution of federal aid to benefit students of moderate financial means as well as those from the most disadvantaged backgrounds.

While the introduction of the Pell Grant program led to substantial increases in the level of grant support from the federal government, the real changes in tuition, room, and board charges during the 1970s were on average negligible (see Figure 2). However, beginning in the early 1980s, college costs rose dramatically, particularly at private institutions. A comparison of Figures 1 and 2 suggests a correlation between higher tuition prices and lower levels of federal support, rather than the reverse.

INSTITUTIONAL RESPONSES TO THE PELL GRANT PROGRAM

A fundamental (and unresolved) question associated with the introduction of the Pell Grant is how institutions adjusted to the infusion of federal grant money with respect to tuition charges, the allocation of financial aid, and the range of course offerings. Evaluation of the outcomes associated with the Pell Grant rests on understanding how the program changed the potential costs of different types of postsecondary education for students from a range of economic and family circumstances. We must look at how this broader set of educational opportunities influenced enrollment and persistence in college.

FIGURE 2.   *Trends in College Costs (in constant 1994 U.S. dollars)*

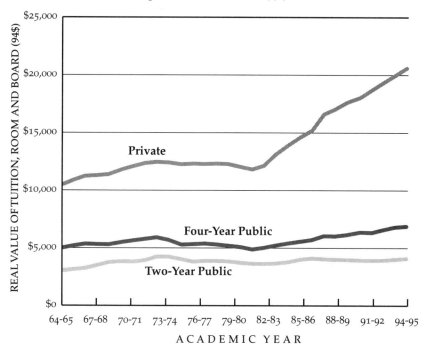

Source: U.S. Department of Education, *The Digest of Education Statistics 1996,* Table 309. "Average undergraduate tuition and fees and room and board rates paid by students in institutions of higher education, by type and control of institution: 1964-65 to 1995-96." Data on total tuition, room, and board costs deflated using the CPI.

For the narrow population of "traditional" college students—those considering college immediately after high school graduation and dependent on their parents for financial assistance—the actual decline in net college costs accompanying the introduction of the Pell Grant may have been somewhat smaller than the statutory Pell Grant maximum, due to changes in institutional policies. Such a hypothesis is not new. In fact, it was advanced in the mid-1980s by former Secretary of Education William Bennett, who argued that the Pell Grant and other Title IV financial aid programs actually served to fuel tuition increases. Yet, as suggested by McPherson and Schapiro,[3] it may be that tuition levels and student aid are linked in the opposite direction if colleges feel obliged to raise tuition to make up for resources lost to declines in federal aid.[4] While the Bennett proposition recognizes the important role of institutional behavior in the delivery of student aid, it misses the key distinction between colleges and universities and profit-maximizing entities.

Much of the market for higher education differs appreciably from the standard competitive paradigm in that many of the participants are either private, not-for-profit, or state-controlled public enterprises. As such, these institutions do not maximize profits. For many of them, the character and diversity of the student body is an important input to the overall education process. These institutions have considerable latitude in determining tuition levels and aid allocations to meet educational objectives. At the most elemental level, the processes determining tuition and the allocation of financial aid are not well-defined. Nevertheless, quite rudimentary models of institutional behavior lead to the conclusion that the introduction of the Pell Grant subsidies would not lead to a dollar-for-dollar reduction in the net cost of college for the target population.[5]

To illustrate, consider two quite extreme cases: a relatively affluent college with an extensive student aid program in place before the introduction of the Pell Grant and a less-affluent college with no appreciable aid program. In the first case, very low-income students received aid awards from institutional resources greater than or equal to the amount of the Pell Grant. With the introduction of the Pell Grant awards, what will be the reduction in net costs for these students? While theory does not give an explicit figure, the answer will most surely be less than the full amount of the Pell Grant. Institutional funds that once went to very needy students might be reallocated to students who have demonstrable need but are ineligible for the Pell Grant, to merit-based aid, or to efforts to reduce the rate of tuition increases. At the other extreme, institutions with no financial aid resources before the initiation of the Pell Grant program will be more constrained in their ability to "undo" the targeting of Pell Grants to low-income students. With the assumption of no change in tuition, students eligible for Pell Grants would see a decline in net costs by the full amount of the Pell Grant award.

Using data on the college costs faced by students before and after the introduction of Pell Grants, we can test the propositions that the reduction in net college costs to students eligible for Pell Grants was equal to the size of the grants and that students from other income groups may have also experienced a decline in net costs with the introduction of the program. Data on high school seniors selecting colleges in the fall of 1972, before the introduction of the Pell Grant, and in 1980 and 1982, after the program had been in place for several years, provide the basis for this analysis. Summaries of regression analyses presented in more detail in Turner consider the change in net costs for representative students from different income levels and at different types of institutions.[6] Table 2 presents the predicted net cost at an institution with a posted tuition of $2,500 for students from four income groups. Between 1972 and 1980, the predicted net cost declined by $983 for students from the lowest-income group, by $870 for students from the next income group, and by $455 for students from the third income group. Treating the subsidy value of loans at one-half the face value leads to relatively larger declines in net cost for students in the most affluent income group. Thus, the punchline from this analysis is that the introduction of the Pell Grant program, as well as

TABLE 2.   *Simulated Grants and Net Costs for Students From Different Income Groups*

| | Grants Only | | Grants + 1/2 Loans | |
| | Tuition Cost=$2,500 | | Tuition Cost=$2,500 | |
	Net Cost	*Grant*	*Net Cost*	*Grant*
Income Group 1, 1972	$1,122	$ 983	$ 867	$1,633
Income Group 1, 1980	139	2,361	−215	2,715
Income Group 1, 1982	173	2,327	−111	2,611
Income Group 2, 1972	1,602	870	1,388	1,112
Income Group 2, 1980	732	1,768	339	2,161
Income Group 2, 1982	925	1,575	590	1,910
Income Group 3, 1972	1,865	455	1,723	777
Income Group 3, 1980	1,410	1,090	947	1,553
Income Group 3, 1982	1,228	1,272	969	1,531
Income Group 4, 1972	2,175	325	2,092	408
Income Group 4, 1980	1,985	515	1,606	894
Income Group 4, 1982	1,972	528	1,793	707

Note: Predicted net costs are calculated using the regression estimates in Sarah E. Turner, "Does Federal Aid Affect College Costs? Evidence from the Pell Program," unpublished paper (1997), which are based on estimates of net cost, defined as tuition minus financial aid for students enrolling in college full time in the fall after high school graduation, from the National Longitudinal Study of the High School Class of 1972 (NLS 72) and High School and Beyond surveys.

Categories for parental income, noted in the table as Income Group 1 to Income Group 4, are based on student-reported parental income as high school seniors. For respondents to the High School and Beyond Survey, Income Group 1 corresponds to income less than $11,999, Income Group 2 is $12,000 to $15,999, Income Group 3 is income between $20,000 and $37,999, and Income Group 4 corresponds to income greater than $38,000. For respondents to the NLS 72 survey, the reported income categories are aligned to best match the categories for 1980 in real terms, though the match is not exact.

corresponding changes in other federal aid policies, was associated with dramatic declines in college costs for low-income students and sizable declines in college costs for students in other income categories.

While there are only limited data at the level of the individual college or university, aggregating institutions by control (public or private) and levels of degrees granted enables basic distinctions between institutions. In brief, private research doctorate institutions show both the largest levels of need-based aid in the initial period and the smallest changes between the 1972 and the 1980 and 1982 cohorts. High school graduates from the lowest income group in 1972 could expect to face a net college cost equal to about 35 cents for each dollar of posted tuition at a private research doctorate institution and a net cost equal to about 63 cents for each dollar of posted tuition at community colleges. By 1980, high school graduates from this low-income group would have faced net college costs of about 15 cents for each dollar of posted tuition at a private research doctorate institution while the additional grant aid led to an expected subsidy above tuition costs for students attending community colleges. Thus, the predicted change in net college costs for students in the lowest-income group is larger in absolute terms (as well as relative to total tuition costs) at community colleges than at private research universities. Yet, students in the second income group, largely students who had demonstrated need but were unlikely to qualify for the maximum Pell award, experienced quite large predicted declines in net college costs between 1972 and 1980 at private research universities. Consideration of the subsidy value of loans has the largest effect on the net cost of college for students in the top two income groups, particularly between 1972 and 1980.

INFLUENCE OF PELL GRANTS ON ENROLLMENT

Because the net cost of college fell for students in the lowest-income group relative to those in the highest-income group, we would expect the enrollment rates for the Pell Grant–eligible population to rise relative to those of other students. Based on the estimates of net cost for grant aid only, the magnitude of the relative enrollment increase for the lowest-income students should have been about four percentage points. If we include the subsidy value of loans in the net cost, we would expect the gain in enrollment for low-income students, relative to students from the highest-income group, to be only about two percentage points. This is well within the confidence intervals of most econometric tests with respect to changes in enrollment associated with the Pell Grant program.

While the available data provide at least a benchmark for measuring the change in net college costs for dependent students from various economic backgrounds, it is much more difficult to make analogous calculations for independent students. Yet it is this population that may well have experienced the most dramatic declines in net college costs with the introduction of the Pell Grant. For older students, the range of postsecondary options is likely to be limited to institutions near their current place of residence and to programs that allow them to balance their other demands, such as work and family. Institutions meeting these criteria are likely to be community colleges and other types of vocational-technical institutions located near an individual's residence or place of work. Given that these institutions had very little discretionary financial aid before the introduction of the Pell Grant program, independent students eligible for Pell Grant funding would be most likely to experience large declines in net cost with the introduction of the program.

It is thus unsurprising that the age groups experiencing the largest increases in enrollment in the wake of the Pell Grant program were not traditional college students but older students. To illustrate this divergence, the top panel of Figure 3 shows the enrollment rate for the 18-to-21-year-old population while the bottom panel shows the rate for those between the ages of 25 and 34. As the top panel shows, the enrollment rate for young people seemed to stagnate with the introduction of the Pell Grant, reflecting other societal forces such as the elimination of the 2-S draft deferment and generally poor economic prospects for college graduates. Yet the introduction of the Pell Grant (partially implemented in 1973 and fully in the subsequent year) was associated with a marked increase in the enrollment rate for individuals in their mid-20s and early-30s. Between 1970 and 1975, the enrollment rate for 25-to-29-year-olds increased by more than one-third, from 7.5 percent to 10.1 percent.

Perhaps the most striking affirmation of the role of the Pell Grant in financing college for non-traditional students is the distribution of Pell Grant awards by age. In academic year 1994-95, there were more independent Pell Grant recipients over the age of 30 than there were dependent student recipients under the age of 20 (see Figure 4). It is hard to discern from the legislative history whether this outcome was envisioned in 1972. But the reality is that the Pell Grant program provides a much

FIGURE 3.   *Changes in Enrollment Rates by Age Group*

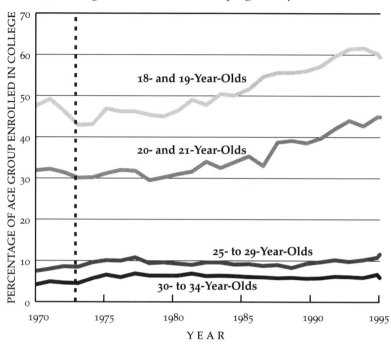

Source: U.S. Department of Education, *The Digest of Education Statistics 1996,* Table 6, "Percent of the population 3 to 34 years old enrolled in school, by age: April 1940 to October 1995."
Note: The vertical line distinguishes the periods before and after the introduction of the Pell Grant program.

larger share of total college costs for the population of nontraditional students than for young people facing educational investments right after high school.

Concomitant with increases in demand by nontraditional students were supply responses by postsecondary institutions. The first such response was the growth in the number of offerings at existing institutions, particularly community colleges and other nonresidential institutions that were well-situated to adapt to the needs of students with families and jobs. For the most part, community colleges adapted to the infusion of funding provided by the Pell Grant through the expansion of existing programs.

Perhaps the least anticipated and most dramatic institutional response to the infusion of Pell Grant funds was the expansion of the for-profit

FIGURE 4. *Distribution of Pell Grant Recipients by Age and Dependency Status, 1994-95*

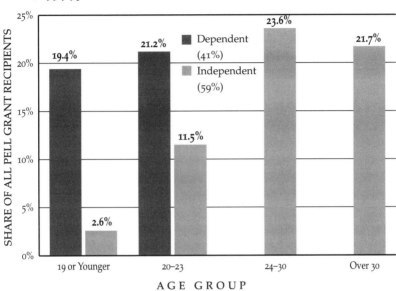

Source: U.S. Department of Education, *1994-95 Title IV Federal Pell Grant Program End-of-Year Report,* Table 11, "Distribution of Federal Pell Grant Recipients by Age and Family Income."

proprietary sector in postsecondary education. For the most part, these institutions specialize in providing vocational or occupational training leading directly to job placement. While the proprietary sector has a long history in U.S. higher education, the expansion associated with the Pell Grant program far exceeded anyone's expectations and was dramatic in scale. The economics fueling this transformation were quite straightforward. Prior to the introduction of the Pell Grant, the only proprietary programs in operation were ones that could attract students at a price equal to the cost of providing the training. The Pell Grant program meant that demand was determined by their cost less the Pell subsidy, leading to a wave of program expansion and the entrance of new institutions into the marketplace.

While the initial share of Pell Grant revenue going to the proprietary sector was modest, about 7 percent of total program expenditures, that share increased rapidly to a peak of over 26 percent of all program revenues in academic year 1987-88 (see Figure 5). In the same year, almost

FIGURE 5.   *Share of Pell Grant Expenditures Going to Recipients in the Proprietary Sector, 1973-74 to 1991-92*

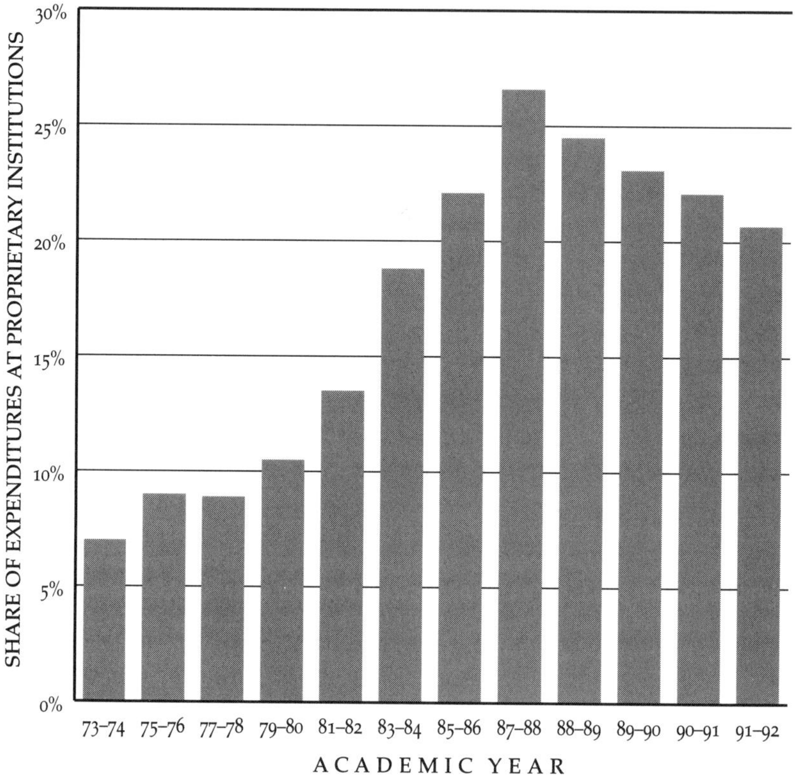

Source: McPherson, Michael and Morton Owen Schapiro, *Keeping College Affordable: Government and Educational Opportunity* (Washington, D.C.: Brookings Institution, 1991), and later issues of the *Federal Pell Grant Program End-of-the-Year Report.*

50 percent of students at proprietary institutions received Pell Grants compared with less than 20 percent of students in the private, nonprofit, and public sectors together.[7]

Research and evaluation efforts have been slower to adapt to this transformation in postsecondary education than the market itself. It was not until 1986, for example, more than a decade after the introduction of the Pell Grant, that proprietary schools were required to complete the Department of Education's annual institutional surveys. Furthermore, labor force surveys of enrollment behavior and educational attainment do not accurately capture the type of training provided at nonbaccalaureate institutions in questions related to degree attainment and years of education completed.

QUESTIONS FOR FUTURE FEDERAL FINANCIAL AID POLICY

Viewed in retrospect, the Pell Grant has had the greatest impact on the segments of postsecondary education that were at the margin of the 1972 legislative process. In particular, institutions in the proprietary sector and students unlikely to seek training in a baccalaureate setting have responded forcefully to the incentives created by the Pell Grant program. Both the growing enrollment rates of students beyond their early twenties and the increasing share of proprietary training in the "outputs" of postsecondary education are evidence to this point. In this context, language changes designed to define the Pell Grant constituency in terms of all postsecondary institutions rather than simply higher education may have been the decisive element determining the outcome of the program.

Focusing narrowly on the enrollment behavior of students in their first years after high school graduation, it is difficult to discern the magnitude of the enrollment response associated with the Pell Grant program. We know, certainly, that in the absence of the program, the total pool of financial aid resources would have been much smaller and, therefore, college costs correspondingly higher. The availability of Pell Grant resources allowed institutions to increase their support for students who were ineligible for Pell Grants but still of limited financial means, and to reduce the net college costs for students eligible for Pell support. This is especially true of baccalaureate-awarding institutions that had financial aid programs already in place at the time the Pell Grant program was introduced.

Reflecting on these quite appreciable changes in the character of postsecondary education since 1972, two sets of questions merit further consideration:

1. The disproportionate increase in enrollment in programs that do not lead to the baccalaureate degree leads to the question of whether the nation has the same interest in subsidizing both baccalaureate and nonbaccalaureate education. To be sure, both types of education are valuable in building the nation's human capital, but does the "one

size fits all" funding approach implicit in the allocation of Pell Grant resources lead to the best outcomes for both individuals and society?

2. In considering how to allocate resources, policymakers must balance the need for rehabilitative investments to train older workers against the need to prepare young workers with a broadly based set of skills that equip them for a rapidly changing labor market. Would greater investments in higher education for individuals at the start of their working lives, particularly targeted at students from the most economically disadvantaged backgrounds, provide a means to increase lifetime economic opportunity and reduce some of the need for education subsidies later in life?

Promoting access to higher education remains one of the few viable policy tools to promote opportunity and reduce intergenerational income inequality. But surprisingly little can be said with certainty about the effectiveness of specific federal financial aid programs in promoting enrollment in college and, perhaps more important, persistence. A combination of better data to address these questions and the renewed interest of academic researchers and policymakers in these questions will be important in shaping the Pell Grant program to function effectively in the twenty-first century.

SARAH E. TURNER *is an assistant professor of education and economics at the University of Virginia. Turner's recent research focuses on the impact of changes in financial aid programs on institutional tuition and aid policies and gender differences in the choice of major and occupational outcomes. She received her B.A. from Princeton University and her Ph.D. in economics from the University of Michigan.*

NOTES

1. Lee W. Hansen, "Economic Growth and Equal Opportunity," in *Education and Economic Productivity*, ed. Edwin Dean (Cambridge, MA: Ballinger, 1984), 89.
2. Michael McPherson and Karl E. Case, "Aid Incentives and Parental Effort: The Impact of Need-Based Aid on Savings and Labor Supply," Wellesley College, unpublished paper (1986).
3. Michael McPherson and Morton Owen Schapiro, "Does Student Aid Affect College Enrollment? New Evidence on a Persistent Controversy," *American Economic Review* 81 (March 1991): 309–18.

4. In *Keeping College Affordable: Government and Educational Opportunity*, (Washington, D.C.: Brookings Institution, 1991), McPherson and Schapiro devote an important chapter to the question of the supply-side effects of student aid. Of particular relevance to this analysis, Appendix C discusses the fungibility of targeted aid with respect to the university's budget constraints and Appendix D explores an empirical model of how changes in external funding affect aid expenditures and tuition pricing. The distinction of the evidence presented in this paper is the focus on the allocation of aid to students from different income strata.

5. The most basic and intuitive model is one in which a monopoly is able to discriminate in price between low-income and high-income consumers (students). A subsidy to low-income students would lead to an increase in the gross price charged to those students and an increase in monopoly profits. This behavior is much like the changes expected in the proprietary sector of postsecondary education, and it may well be that much of the increase in the number of proprietary schools in the late 1970s was associated with the increased profit opportunities provided as a result of the Pell Grant program.

6. Sarah E. Turner, "Does Federal Aid Affect College Costs? Evidence from the Pell Program," unpublished paper (1997).

7. U.S. Department of Education, *The Digest of Education Statistics 1996*, Table 315, "Undergraduates Enrolled Full-time and Part-time in 1992, by Federal Aid Program and by Control and Level of Institution: 1992-93."

The Impact of Pell Grants on Student Persistence in College

John B. Lee

Abstract. *Pell Grants help students from the least advantaged backgrounds not just to gain access, but also to succeed in college. Pell Grant recipients have a persistence rate only eight percentage points lower than undergraduates who did not receive a Pell Grant. Given the barriers to graduation faced by these low-income and at-risk students, this is an encouraging finding. Pell Grants cannot compensate for all the factors that account for student persistence, but they provide a vital foundation for undergraduates with need. The program should be modified to improve persistence by providing a bonus to students who complete college preparatory requirements in high school, front-loading the grants (boosting the Pell Grant amount for undergraduates in their first year of enrollment), and providing an incentive payment to institutions for each Pell Grant recipient who succeeds.*

Financial access to postsecondary education is now nearly universal in the United States. It is possible for most high school graduates who want to continue their education after high school to find, through student aid and reasonable self-help, enough money to enroll in a postsecondary institution. The Pell Grant program is an important part of this achievement.

Improving access to college for low-income students was a primary reason for establishing the Pell Grant program in 1972, but this goal is only part of the picture today. Graduation from college has become an increasingly important measure of educational success. The current emphasis placed by state and national funding sources on student outcomes and institutional accountability focuses on student graduation rates as a prominent indicator of institutional performance. Therefore, the contribution of Pell Grants to the successful completion of a postsecondary program is a more serious question than in the past. If Pell Grants and other student aid programs cannot be shown to contribute to successful student outcomes, they run the risk of losing out in the appropriations battle.

STUDENTS AT RISK OF DROPPING OUT

Since World War II, the share of the population attending college has increased dramatically, but the graduation rate of those enrolled has remained constant at around 50 percent. In the most recent estimates, less than half (46 percent) of those who started college with the goal of attaining a bachelor's degree had completed a degree five years later. Eight percent completed another degree or certificate, for a total of 54 percent completing a degree within five years.[1]

Table 1 shows that low-income students have a smaller chance of graduating than higher-income students. College enrollees from families with incomes below $20,000 have a completion rate 25 percentage points below students with family incomes of $60,000 or more.

We should not conclude that coming from a low-income family is the only impediment to graduation. Horn and Premo identified seven risk factors that decreased students' chances of completing a postsecondary

TABLE 1. *Graduation Rates Five Years After Initial Enrollment of Students Who Were Seeking a Bachelor's Degree at the Time of First Enrollment*

Family Income (Dependent Students)	Bachelor's Degree	Total (any degree)
Less than $20,000	37%	43%
$20,000-$39,999	43%	53%
$40,000-$59,999	49%	57%
$60,000 or more	61%	68%

Source: National Center for Education Statistics, *The Condition of Education* (Washington, D.C.: U.S. Department of Education, 1996).

TABLE 2. *Percentage of Undergraduates Experiencing Risk Factors That Reduce Their Chances of Graduating*

Risk Factor	Percentage of Undergraduates
Delayed enrollment	43%
Enrolled part-time	54%
Financially independent	52%
Have dependents	22%
Work full-time	37%
Single parent	8%
Did not graduate from high school	6%

Source: L. Horn and M. Premo, *Profile of Undergraduates in U.S. Postsecondary Education Institutions: 1992-93* (Washington, D.C.: U.S. Department of Education, 1995).

education (see Table 2).[2] These included social, economic, educational, and enrollment variables. Approximately 70 percent of enrolled undergraduates experienced at least one of these risk factors.

Many students experienced multiple risk factors, and the higher the number of risk factors, the lower their chance of graduating. Undergraduates with no risk factors were twice as likely to have attained a degree or be enrolled at the end of five years than students with three or more risk factors.

Two of the risk factors also reduce the chances of a student receiving a Pell Grant. First, students who work full-time and enroll part-time reduce their chances of qualifying for a Pell Grant because working full-time increases income and attending college part-time reduces costs. Second, students with children are also less likely to receive a Pell Grant. This is partially attributable to the fact that students with children are more likely to attend part-time. In addition, many are married and their joint household income puts them out of the eligibility range for Pell Grants.

Both dependent and independent students establish eligibility for Pell Grants based on their current financial strength, but they represent different types of academic risk. Independent students have a higher risk of dropping out because of a number of factors: they tend to enroll part-time, delay starting college immediately after high school, have dependents, work full-time while enrolled, and they are more likely to be single parents with family obligations that make demands on their income and time. Students who are financially independent cannot count on their parents as much as dependent students can to help them during life's small emergencies. In fact, persevering to graduation represents as much of a struggle for independent students with these risk factors as starting college in the first place. In addition, independent students, as well as other students at risk of dropping out, are likely to be more sensitive to the rising cost of attendance than students without risk.

Research has uncovered other correlates of persistence besides the previously mentioned risk factors. Not surprisingly, many of these suggest that students with the best chance of succeeding in college come from families that have economic and educational advantages. The following factors are correlated with attaining a bachelor's degree within five years:[3]

- being female,
- being white or Asian,
- being single when starting college,

- being from the highest socioeconomic status (SES) quartile,

- having parents with advanced degrees, and

- starting college at a four-year institution.

Other predictors of persistence include encouragement from family and friends, institutional support (including student aid), and the student's commitment to his or her goal.[4] These findings suggest that both institutions and families can make important contributions toward improving student persistence.

The relationship between income and risk is not direct, but the evidence still suggests that low-income students have less chance of graduating from college than higher-income students. The research is consistent in confirming that student aid makes a small but positive contribution to improving student persistence. This conservative finding may be due to the fact that the research on persistence includes all student aid. Pell Grants do more to help students persist than student aid overall because those with the greatest financial need are most sensitive to the cost of attendance. Pell Grant-eligible students often need more than just financial assistance to succeed in college, but the Pell Grant award does help.

ACADEMIC PREPARATION

Measures of academic preparation in high school provide the best predictors of student persistence in college. This is hardly surprising, but it is important because measures of academic ability correlate with family income. The following three factors measure overlapping predictors of student persistence:[5]

- Students who took a college preparatory curriculum in high school have a better chance of persisting in college.

- Students with high grades in high school and college have higher persistence rates in college than those with lower grades.

- Students with high college admission test scores are more likely to persist in college than those with lower scores.

Because academic preparation is so important to success in college, little argument can be made against the proposition that any effort to improve the educational preparation of low-income students should improve their persistence rates in college. Federally funded programs such as Talent Search and Upward Bound exemplify approaches designed to increase low-income student achievement by preparing them for the rigors of college study.

INSTITUTIONAL SUPPORT

Student persistence is not totally a function of student and family background. Colleges and universities can have a major effect. Colleges, especially those enrolling a significant number of students with at-risk characteristics, can provide support programs to improve retention. Bean and Metzner described some of the things institutions can do to address the external factors that might derail a student, in particular, nonschool responsibilities that can interfere with attendance.[6] Offering child care, scheduling classes at hours compatible with work schedules, and providing transportation options may be generally helpful. One college reported that simply calling students on the telephone when they failed to attend class improved retention rates significantly.

Most research suggests that students have a greater chance of graduating if they take advantage of support services on campus and participate fully in college life. For example, students who visit the counselor's office or spend time in the library have a better chance of graduating than those who do not. Participation in summer orientation programs and living on campus improved student persistence,[7] and interaction with faculty members outside class and greater involvement in classroom activities also improved persistence.[8]

Indeed, a student's integration into campus life is an important predictor of persistence. Students who work more than part-time while attending school part-time reduce their chances to interact with other students and to share experiences outside of class. These students may thus have a lower chance of graduating compared with those who work 20 hours a week or less.[9] Working long hours not only takes time and energy away from study but also draws a student's attention away from involvement in the educational environment. This loss of connection with campus life may be detrimental to success. Tinto found that persistence improved if students were integrated into the life of the institution and that a heavy work schedule interfered with participation in campus activities.[10]

INSTITUTIONAL TYPE

Many studies of student persistence do not consider differences between types of institutions or types of degrees. Different correlates of persistence are found for students seeking an academic degree (bachelor's or associate's degree) compared with those seeking a certificate.[11]

We know, for example, that a student who initially enrolls in a four-year institution is more likely to receive a bachelor's degree than a student who enrolls in a community college and plans to transfer. This is true even when relevant background variables are held constant,[12] and may be related to factors such as the lack of a campus-centered social experience at community colleges, the complications of transferring to a new institution, and/or the unwillingness of the new institution to accept all the community college credits. But it is also important to note that community college students who transfer successfully have the same chance of graduating as those who started at a four-year college.

Persistence rates decline at both two- and four-year colleges as the number of student risk factors increases. However, the presence of these factors did not affect the persistence and attainment of students attending less-than-two-year vocational institutions.[13] And, as expected, the data show that two-year colleges and vocational-technical schools enroll a greater share of students with multiple risk factors than four-year colleges do.

Based on the analysis of Beginning Postsecondary Students (BPS) data from the U.S. Department of Education, the correlates of persistence were different for students seeking a certificate than for those aspiring to a bachelor's degree.[14] This is important because low-income students are more likely to seek a vocational certificate than higher-income students. While attending full-time and enrolling in postsecondary education immediately after high school were related to receiving a certificate, all the other factors related to attaining a bachelor's degree had either a neutral or an opposite effect on such students. For example, students seeking a certificate who enrolled at less-than-two-year institutions were more likely to succeed than students enrolling in longer programs. Another finding that was inconsistent with those for academic programs was that Hispanic students were more successful than others. And family background variables such as income did not predict student success in vocational-technical education.

St. John et al. examined persistence of students in proprietary schools and found that African-American and Hispanic students were more likely to persist than white students.[15] They also reported that students who had not completed high school or had a GED were more likely to persist than those with a high school diploma. Moreover, unlike students seeking bachelor's degrees, family income had no relationship to graduation rates for students at proprietary schools. Again, these findings suggest that different factors predict success in technical and vocational programs than in academic programs.

EFFECTS OF DIFFERENT TYPES OF STUDENT AID ON PERSISTENCE

Researchers agree that receiving a grant improves the probability of completing a degree. The effect of loans and work-study on student persistence generates more debate. Indeed, Thomas[16] (as reported in Swail[17]) suggested that loans made to minority students may even have a negative influence on persistence because such students fear financial indebtedness.

Other financial factors in addition to student aid must be considered in the persistence equation, however. For example, the net price of attendance (the cost of attendance minus student aid) may be the key indicator, rather than the amount of aid by itself. Another part of the equation is the family contribution. Porter suggested that family financial support, tuition charges, and amount of aid are important predictors of student persistence, at least at independent colleges.[18] Student aid and family contribution are less important in predicting persistence at public institutions because of the lower cost of attendance.

St. John et al. found that student aid had a modest but positive association with retention for students at proprietary institutions.[19] But a more important predictor of continuing proprietary school enrollment than aid by itself is the amount of unmet need. This may reflect the fact that compared with other sectors, proprietary institutions enroll a higher proportion of low-income students who pay high tuition charges.

These studies suggest that whatever the source or type, financial aid must be adequate to encourage continued enrollment. Simply receiving aid does not improve persistence if the amount does not cover enough of the student's cost of attendance.

In addition, student aid may influence persistence differently in each progressive year of the undergraduate experience. Several legislative efforts have been made to introduce front-loaded Pell Grants so that first-

and second-year students would be eligible for larger grants than upper-division students, who would be offered more loan assistance. Research shows the benefits of this approach. St. John found that while both grants and loans improved persistence, grants had a more positive effect in the first year of college, while loans were more productive during the later years.[20] Using a different approach, the General Accounting Office reported that grants reduced the dropout rate for low-income students but loans did not.[21] It agreed with St. John that grant aid awarded in the first year of attendance was more effective than in later years.

Murdock, Nix-Mayer, and Tsui also reported that grant assistance was effective in promoting student retention during the first year of enrollment in college.[22] They found that students who received grants in their first year at a four-year institution were more likely to continue than those who did not receive a grant. This was especially true for African-American students. Ninety percent of the students who received a grant continued their education in the second year compared with 75 percent of those with no grant. Reducing unmet need and increasing the amount of student aid improved persistence from the sophomore to the junior year and from the junior to the senior year. Higher awards and lower unmet need resulted in better retention throughout the college years.[23]

In another study, St. John, Kirshstein, and Noell[24] reported that, in general, financial aid was positively associated with persistence, but that different factors were associated with persistence in different academic years. These findings suggest that students are more sensitive to cost early in their college careers. Student aid is only one component of a student's financial picture, and the research literature is consistent in reporting that financial aid alone is not sufficient to keep students in college. The student's commitment, support from significant others, and compatibility with an institution's academic and social environment are important in explaining college persistence.[25]

PELL GRANTS AND PERSISTENCE

Disentangling the impact of Pell Grants from the effects of student aid in general is difficult. Financial aid administrators generally package Pell Grants with other sources of aid, which makes it hard to determine whether it is the overall aid package or a particular element of the package that accounts for persistence. Few studies have attempted to isolate the effects of Pell Grants from other aid.

The data in Table 3 suggest, however, that Pell Grants have a positive relationship with persistence. Table 3 reports the percentage of undergraduates who first enrolled at least half time in 1989-90 and who either graduated or were still enrolled in 1994-95. Students who enrolled less than half time were not included because they were not eligible for a Pell Grant. Those who were still enrolled or had graduated were defined as persisting students.

As a group, undergraduates who received a Pell Grant were slightly less likely to continue their enrollment than those who did not (61 percent versus 69 percent). This is not surprising given the enormous advantage higher-income students have over students from lower-income backgrounds. However, the findings provide compelling evidence that Pell Grants made a positive difference in the persistence of undergraduates from the lowest two socioeconomic (SES) quartiles. Socioeconomic status reflects a combination of family income, educational achievement, and parents' job responsibilities at the time the student first enrolled. Pell Grants make it possible for students from the least-advantaged backgrounds to succeed in college. Students from the lowest SES quartile (the first quartile) significantly improved their chances of persisting if they received a Pell Grant.

TABLE 3. *Percentage of Undergraduates Who Persisted With or Without a Pell Grant, 1989-90 to 1994-95*

Characteristics	No Pell	Pell
Total	69%	61%
Socioeconomic status (1990)		
First quartile	47%	55%
Second quartile	58%	61%
Third and Fourth quartiles	72%	65%
First enrolled at 22 years of age or less	70%	62%
First enrolled at 23 years of age or more	47%	55%
High school diploma	70%	61%
No high school diploma	35%	55%
Independent	52%	52%
Dependent	76%	69%
Have children	44%	52%
No children	70%	69%

Source: National Center for Education Statistics, *Beginning Postsecondary Students, 1989-90 to 1994-95.* Second-Student Follow-Up Data Set.

Table 3 also suggests that students with other risk factors increased their chances of persisting if they received a Pell Grant. Students who enrolled at age 23 or older, had no high school diploma, were independent, or had children all increased their chances of persisting if they received a Pell Grant. In other words, Pell Grants appeared to help those students who face the greatest risk of dropping out of college.

Overall, students who did not receive a Pell Grant had a persistence rate only 8 percent higher than those who did. Given the other barriers to graduation experienced by low-income students and those most at risk of dropping out, this is a gratifying finding. Pell Grants may not compensate for all the risk factors, but they provide a vital foundation for students with need.

CONCLUSION

Pell Grants appear to improve the graduation rates of low-income students and those most at risk of dropping out of college. Indeed, students with the most need show the greatest improvement in persistence with the help of Pell Grants, which allow students to make educational choices that increase the odds of completing their programs successfully. For example, a Pell Grant may allow a student to attend college full-time immediately after high school instead of delaying enrollment to earn money or attending part-time while working full-time.

The data also show that Pell Grants provide a major resource for helping students complete a vocational-technical degree or certificate. The evidence suggests that students who might be predicted to drop out of academic programs may be more successful in vocational programs. More consideration should be given to helping students with inadequate academic preparation understand that choosing technical or vocational programs may improve their chances of graduating.

POLICY RECOMMENDATIONS

No single approach to improving persistence will be successful by itself. To encourage significant improvement in educational outcomes for low-income students, all facets of the problem need to be addressed and the Pell Grants address only one. Improving the persistence rates of at-risk students requires providing adequate academic preparation before enroll-ment and meaningful institutional support once students arrive on cam-pus. Nevertheless, several changes to the Pell Grant program would help improve the prospects of grant recipients.

Increase the maximum Pell Grant for first-year students.

We have seen that grant aid has the most beneficial effect on persistence in the first year of college. Therefore, increasing the maximum Pell Grant, especially for students early in their academic careers, would likely improve persistence rates. After a successful first year of postsecondary education, students have an improved chance of graduating. Requiring loans in the first year of college decreases student persistence, while increasing loan assistance after the first year does not have a demon-strably negative effect on persistence. The reason for this is that students who continue after their first year may perceive a greater likelihood of success and be more willing to borrow in the succeeding years. A sec-ondary effect of this approach would be to reduce the student loan default rate attributed to first-year dropouts. The changes could be designed so that a graduating student would leave college with the same proportion of loan to grant assistance as is currently the case. The only differences would be the improved persistence rate of low-income students and lower default rates.

Require participation in precollege preparation programs for Pell Grant eligibility.

Increased grant assistance should be combined with effective precollege preparation. Merisotis et al. suggested tying increased grant assistance to participation in supplementary precollege educational programs.[26] This premium could provide an incentive for at-risk students to make an extra effort to prepare themselves for college. This would also encour-age high schools that serve a high proportion of low-income students to offer college preparatory programs.

A simplified version of this approach would be to reward low-income high school students who complete all the entrance requirements for the state's public flagship university with a large Pell Grant. This approach would put states in a position to define program standards and monitor student progress and would also keep the federal government out of the job of defining educational standards. This large grant should be substantial enough to make a difference to the student and motivate high schools to make sure their students have access to all the required classes.

Such an approach would not provide immediate help for adult students who want to return to college. Nor would it recognize the nonacademic achievement of vocational students or students in the performing arts who wish to enroll in postsecondary institutions. But for high school students wishing to enter academic programs, improved preparation tied to Pell Grant eligibility would likely increase persistence rates.

Provide improved counseling and information.

Students and their families must have the information to help make the appropriate institutional choice. This goes beyond simply evaluating students' academic credentials or calculating the amount of the financial aid package they might receive. Students could make better educational decisions if they understood, for example, that they have a smaller chance of succeeding when they delay entry into college or enroll part-time and work full-time while attending. Potential students should be given accurate and realistic information about the risks inherent in their enrollment decisions. They may not be aware that certain short-term, money-saving choices reduce their chances of graduating.

Expand on-campus support programs for Pell Grant recipients.

Once at-risk students enroll, postsecondary institutions must provide supportive programs that help integrate newcomers into college life. Colleges also need to provide services to help these students cope with the many problems that can derail their educational plans. Orientation programs, study-skill classes, tutorial help, day care, and transportation assistance can boost persistence.

An incentive paid to institutions for each year completed by Pell Grant recipients would spur colleges and universities to implement programs for improving the persistence of low-income students. Even a small incentive might encourage institutions to be more sensitive to the needs of such students.

THE FUTURE

The first 25 years of the Pell Grant program have made college possible for a generation of students. Improving student persistence has always been secondary to the goal of helping low-income students enroll in college. So it is a bonus that Pell Grants appear to improve the likelihood of graduation for many students who had to overcome multiple impediments to success. Student success in college should be the overriding goal of the Pell Grant, and the research on persistence has defined some new challenges for this enduring program.

JOHN B. LEE *is the president of JBL Associates, Inc., in Bethesda, Maryland. He started JBL 12 years ago and specializes in projects concerned with local, state, and national postsecondary policy issues. Lee's prior career included service as a staff member for the House Education and Labor Committee, a community college teacher, and a member of the staff of the Education Commission of the States in Denver, Colorado. He received his Ed.D. degree from the University of California, Berkeley.*

NOTES

1. National Center for Education Statistics, *The Condition of Education* (Washington, D.C.: U.S. Department of Education, 1996).
2. L. Horn and M. Premo, *Profile of Undergraduates in U.S. Postsecondary Education Institutions: 1992-93.* (Washington, D.C.: U.S. Department of Education, Office of Educational Research and Improvement, National Center for Education Statistic, October 1995).
3. National Center for Education Statistics, *The Condition of Education.*
4. Alberto F. Cabrera, Nora Amaury, and Maria B. Castaneda, "College Persistence: Structural Equations Modeling Test of an Integrated Model of Student Retention," *Journal of Higher Education* 64 (2) (March/April 1993).
5. G. R. Hanson and D. M. Swann, "Using Multiple Program Impact Analysis to Document Institutional Effectiveness," *Research in Higher Education* 34 (February 1993): 71–94.
6. J. Bean and M. Metzner, "A Conceptual Model of Nontraditional Undergraduate Student Attrition," *Review of Educational Research* 55 (4) (1985).
7. G. R. Hanson and D. M. Swann.
8. J. Grossit, "Patterns of Integration, Commitment, Student Characteristics, and Retention Among Younger and Older Students," *Research in Higher Education* 32 (April 1991): 159–78.
9. J. Naretto, "Adult Student Retention: The Influence of Internal and External Communities," *NASPA Journal* 32 (Winter 1995): 90–97.
10. V. Tinto, "Sociological View of Student Persistence," Presented at the Seventh Annual NASSGP/NCHELP Research Network, Washington, D.C., 1990.
11. National Center for Education Statistics, *The Condition of Education.*

12. K. Dougherty, "Community Colleges and Baccalaureate Attainment," *Journal of Higher Education* 63 (March/April 1992): 188–214.

13. L. Berkner, S. Cuccaro-Alamin, and A. McCormick, *Descriptive Summary of 1989-90 Beginning Students: Five Years Later* (Washington, D.C.: U.S. Department of Education, National Center for Education Statistics, 1996).

14. Ibid.

15. E. St. John, J. Starkey, M. Paulsen, and L. Mdaduagha, "The Influence of Prices and Price Subsidies on Within-Year Persistence by Students in Proprietary Schools," *Educational Evaluation and Policy Analysis* 17 (2) (Summer 1995): 149–65.

16. G. Thomas, "The Access and Success of Blacks and Latinos in U.S. Graduate and Professional Education," a working paper prepared for the National Research Council, 1986.

17. W. Scott Swail, "A Conceptual Framework for Student Retention in Science, Engineering, & Mathematics Programs," Dissertation, School of Education and Human Development of George Washington University, Washington, D.C., 1995.

18. O. Porter, "Persistence in Four-year Colleges: Are There Differences in Public and Independent Institutions?" Preliminary Findings of a Path Analysis presented at the NASSGP/NCHELP Research Network, Washington, D.C., May 1990.

19. E. St. John, J. Starkey, M. Paulsen, and L. Mdaduagha.

20. E. St. John, "Price Response in Persistence Decisions: An Analysis of the High School and Beyond Senior Cohort," presented at the NASSGP/NCHELP Research Network, Washington, D.C., May 1990.

21. General Accounting Office, *Higher Education: Restructuring Student Aid Could Reduce Low-Income Student Dropout Rate,* Washington, D.C., 1995.

22. T. Murdock, L. Nix-Mayer, and P. Tsui, "The Effect of Types of Student Aid on Student Persistence Towards Graduation," paper read at Association for Institutional Research, Boston, Mass, May 1995. (Quoted in *Higher Education Abstracts* 31 (2): Winter 1996).

23. Ibid.

24. E. St. John, R. J. Kirshstein, and J. Noell, "The Effects of Student Financial Aid on Persistence: A Sequential Analysis," *Review of Higher Education* 14 (3) (Spring 1991): 383–406.

25. Alberto Cabrera, J. Stampen, and W. L. Hansen, "Exploring the Effects of Ability to Pay on Persistence in College," *Review of Higher Education* 13 (3) (Spring 1990): 303–36.

26. J. Merisotis, C. O'Brien, A. Gray, M. Hill, and C. Richardson, *The Next Step: Student Aid for Student Success* (Boston, MA: The Education Resources Institute, June 1995).

The Voucher That Works: The Role of Pell Grants in Welfare, Employment, and Job Training Policies

Anthony P. Carnevale
and Louis S. Jacobson

Abstract. *Pell Grants and student loans have become a key component in the nation's patchwork of workforce development programs. Federal student aid is the predominant and most effective vehicle for delivering classroom training to two critical populations: welfare recipients and dislocated workers. The use of Pell Grants to increase the employability and earnings prospects of disadvantaged populations is part of the expanding economic role of postsecondary education. Yet the Pell Grant program has fallen far short of its potential because too many individuals do not know of its existence or are unduly reluctant to apply for the aid. And many individuals leave school too quickly because they underestimate the importance of getting their certificates or degrees. The key missing components are better information about the career-enhancing returns from postsecondary education and better methods for delivering that information.*

Over the past quarter century, Pell Grants have emerged as the dominant provider of high-quality, low-cost education and training not only for low-income college students in general but also for dislocated workers, welfare families, and other nontraditional students. The Pell Grant, along with student loans, has gradually become the nation's all-purpose education and training voucher and a critical element in the nation's employment and welfare policies. According to the U.S. Department of Education, currently almost 322,000 welfare mothers, 122,555 of their dependent children, and about 75,000 dislocated workers are Pell Grant recipients; 48 percent of dislocated workers receiving Pell Grants also get student loans.[1]

The use of Pell Grants and student loans to increase the employabili-ty of welfare mothers and dislocated workers is part of the expanding economic role of postsecondary education, which has become the main qualification for high-skill, high-wage, entry-level jobs in the United States.

While our efforts to educate a world-class workforce have increas-ingly relied on postsecondary institutions, even with the availability of Pell Grants many of the disadvantaged have been left behind. Workers who fall out of the "first-chance" education and training system, often with poor information about the outcomes of their educational choices, can face grim employment and earnings prospects. Low-skilled work-ers have increasingly borne the burden of falling real wages in an era of rising income inequality, resulting from an economy that increasingly rewards skill and credentials in the work place. Even low-skill workers who try to reenter the first-chance system, or decide to try the "second-chance" public job training programs, often see little improvement in their relative position if they do not choose wisely among their educa-tion and training options. While Pell Grants are an essential piece of the employment and education policy pie, information is the ingredient that holds the pie together. An information strategy that disseminates the economic costs and benefits of particular educational paths is essential in creating an employment system that aims to provide workers with the means to secure a job with a living wage.

OUR PRAGMATIC PAST

The pragmatic bias in U.S. higher education is nothing new. Postsecondary institutions always have had a primary economic role in career devel-opment. Our earliest colleges were created to provide vocational train-ing, principally to teachers and preachers. The land-grant universities were initiated in response to the skill needs of the industrial revolution as well as to improve agricultural productivity and develop an officer corps to lead federal military forces. The GI Bill was enacted to facilitate reentry into the civilian workforce of military personnel mobilized for World War II, and the National Defense Education Act was created to meet cold war needs in science and engineering. Cooperative education programs—our version of postsecondary apprenticeship programs—are well established in U.S. higher education. Currently, the vast majority of associate's degrees and certificates are vocationally oriented, and roughly 80 percent of bachelor's degrees are in applied or vocational fields.[2] The phenomenal growth in the number of adults pursuing post-secondary education has been driven primarily by work-related skill needs. Study in graduate and professional degree programs is intended to further prepare students for work in specific occupations and professional fields. Moreover, changing labor markets tend to drive course enrollments, as is evident in the recent shift from liberal arts to business and professional courses of study.[3]

The role of postsecondary institutions in preparing individuals for careers has expanded in the latter half of this century. This expansion can be divided into five overlapping phases that reflect the complex interplay between the supply and demand for college-educated workers.

Phase 1: The vocational role of postsecondary institutions surged in the post-World War II era as a result of the new demand for skilled labor caused by the economic boom between 1946 and 1973 and the increased supply of highly qualified students generated, in part, by the GI Bill.

Phase 2: By the early 1970s, the postwar baby boom generation met and then exceeded the demand for college-educated workers. The baby boomers—the 78 million Americans born between 1946 and 1964—began crowding the college pipeline in 1964, continuing to populate college campuses until 1984, by which time most had graduated. Once in the labor market, the sudden oversupply of well-educated but inexperienced boomers, in combination with the end of the postwar boom and the beginning of the "stagflation" in the 1970s, reduced the earnings of college graduates relative to high school graduates.

Phase 3: The demographically induced demand for postsecondary education declined after 1980. "Generation X"—people born between 1964 and 1982—produced only two-thirds as many births as the baby boom. The drop-off in the number of births, along with the decline in the earnings of college graduates relative to high school graduates in the 1970s, slowed the enrollment of traditional college-age students.

Phase 4: The reduction in enrollment of traditional college-age students was offset by a surge in enrollments by adults and other nontraditional students.[4] The surge in nontraditional students reflected the muted but steady increase in the demand for lifelong learning in the new economy and the aging of baby boomers.

Phase 5: The relative economic value of a college education over a high school degree reasserted itself in the early 1980s as inflation disappeared and the restructuring of business organizations began in earnest. Low inflation meant employers were paying real dollars for labor, giving them incentives to hire fewer but more highly skilled workers instead of many low-skilled workers.

In addition, as investments flowed to low-wage areas, particularly Southeast Asia, low-skilled but highly paid U.S. workers lost jobs and experienced large wage declines. Growth and competition also encouraged the restructuring of business organizations into flexible institutional networks driven by outcome standards. The new flexible networks required more computer-based technology. Flexible institutional formats and technologies required more workers with a postsecondary education. As a result, since 1983 the value of a college education relative to a high school degree has been rising continuously.

As we look into the next century, both the demographic and economic demand for postsecondary education will increase simultaneously. The continuing restructuring of the economy suggests a continuing demand for college-educated workers.[5] Generation Y—people born after 1981—so far constitutes about 58 million births, 20 million less than the baby boom but 2 million more than the Generation X cohort. The oldest of Generation Y are just turning 16 and getting ready to go to college. This new cohort should produce a younger and more diverse college population, starting in 1998 and ending in 2015 when the last of them graduates.[6]

During the postwar period, the economic role of postsecondary education has expanded into job-related learning in four domains, each further removed from postsecondary education's traditional academic role and its traditional 18-to-24-year-old middle-class client base.

First, with the gradual disappearance of good jobs that required only high school or less, postsecondary education has become more important in providing a "first chance" at good jobs for the vast majority of high school graduates.

Second, postsecondary education has become second only to learning on the job as a means of upgrading the skills of employed adults.

Third, postsecondary institutions, especially community colleges and proprietary schools, have become the principal providers of education and training for "second chance" clients who dropped out or missed out on their first chance at building a solid educational foundation for work.

Fourth, postsecondary institutions have become the primary education and training providers for workers who have been dislocated by economic and technological change and whose skills are insufficient to allow them to find new jobs, especially jobs that will eventually provide them with earnings comparable to the jobs they lost.

In general, the growth of more applied options in higher education has increased access for low-income students and adult workers. Almost 70 percent of postsecondary students in the lowest income quartile attend two-year colleges and proprietary schools, and 20 percent graduate, compared with the 7 percent of low-income students who graduate from four-year institutions and graduate or professional schools.[7] Currently, over 40 percent of postsecondary students are adults pursuing career goals. The expansion of postsecondary institutions into more applied areas also has resulted in a more diverse student population, preparing the way for the coming waves of ethnic and racial diversity throughout postsecondary education.

THE SILENT PARTNERSHIP

The broadening of postsecondary institutions to serve social welfare and employment policy is at the frontier of the expanding economic role of higher education. It is the latest wrinkle in the long history of pragmatism in U.S. education. Yet in spite of its contributions, in practice student aid largely is perceived by policymakers as a separate system with little connection to or value for the conglomeration of welfare reform and employment and training efforts of the state and federal governments.

The silent partnership between student aid, welfare reform, and employment policy has evolved as an ad hoc collaboration that stems from the interplay between the growing economic importance of postsecondary education and the unique structure of the U.S. education and job training systems. It is hardly news that jobs for those with only a high school education do not pay high wages and are disappearing. Postsecondary education and training facilitate success in the new skill-based economy. Those with postsecondary degrees have access to managerial, professional, and technical occupations, which, in turn, provide access to training and technology on the job that increase their earnings advantages even further.[8]

In the United States, postsecondary institutions have expanded to meet job-related training needs, in part because there is nowhere else to turn. The structure of education and training in the United States is unique.

Unlike Europe and Asia, where employers, unions, and governments play a stronger role in providing job-related learning, the U.S. job preparation and retraining system relies to a much greater extent on educational institutions to prepare people for work and to provide lifelong learning. In Europe, there are two distinctive education and training tracks into the new economy: Europeans can choose between college and company-based apprenticeships that mix education and training. But in the United States, tracking violates egalitarian values. As a result, our one-track system has been forced to adapt to serve new education and training needs.

Postsecondary institutions have expanded their role in providing job-related learning in part because they have gradually taken on education and training missions left behind by failed attempts to build alternative systems to educate and train disadvantaged and dislocated workers. Attempts to create an alternative "school-to-work apprenticeship" system for noncollege youth, as well as attempts to expand employer-based training and to build a second chance training system for educationally disadvantaged and dislocated workers, have been made but have not taken root in the United States. This leaves postsecondary institutions as both the nation's principal educator and job trainer.

The inherent adaptability of U.S. postsecondary institutions also has facilitated expansion to meet new job-related learning demands. The system is highly decentralized and market-driven, with relatively few barriers to entry for new providers. The $35 billion in federal grants and loans and the additional $10 billion in tax subsidies for families empower families and individual students to make their own choices between the more than 1,500 two-year colleges, 2,200 four-year institutions, and 5,000 proprietary schools. And students and families do make choices: about one-third of the postsecondary institutions lose enrollments each year even though overall enrollments have continued to increase.[9]

EDUCATIONAL QUALITY VERSUS ACCESS

The expanding economic role of higher education creates tensions between educational quality and access for nontraditional students. Tension between high standards and access is perennial in higher education policy. Funding for "fly-by-night" schools was first investigated by Congress in the early 1950s when concern emerged over abuses in the use of the GI Bill. The

Higher Education Act of 1965, which established the first broadly based student aid programs sponsored by the federal government, separated academic and vocational training based on experience with the GI Bill. In the 1970s, however, students in all two- and four-year institutions and most proprietary schools became eligible for the full range of federal higher education grants and loans, including students who were not high school graduates but could demonstrate some "ability to benefit." Later, concern over the quality of postsecondary education reemerged as nondegree students made up a growing share of grant and loan recipients and lagging completion rates and loan defaults followed. The result has been a long-standing tug-of-war between federal education authorities and providers over appropriate performance standards for nondegree institutions and assessments to qualify students without high school diplomas for student aid.[10] The current emphasis on cost and accountability in the higher education dialogue promises even more intense debates over performance standards for institutions and the appropriate use of tests to determine whether students without high school diplomas have enough ability to benefit from college courses.

Policymakers are right to be concerned about the quality of learning in postsecondary institutions. As the importance of access to postsecondary education grows and accreditation and certification extend to a greater diversity of institutions, quality standards may well be compromised. This could happen in much the same way that near universal access and a graduation rate approaching 90 percent in U.S. high schools have diluted the value and the quality of the high school diploma.[11] There is similar evidence of emerging quality problems in higher education. The struggle to maintain quality while extending public financial assistance to proprietary schools is the most obvious case in point, but the problem exists in all types of postsecondary institutions.

The growing disparity in the quality of postsecondary degrees also is blamed, in part, for the parallel growth in the disparity of earnings and occupational options for postsecondary graduates. For instance, the proportion of four-year college graduates who were working in jobs in which the average educational level of workers was a high school diploma or less increased from 7.1 percent in 1971 to 10.1 percent in 1995. Over the same period, the proportion of four-year college graduates working in jobs in which the average educational level of workers was 13 years or less increased from 23.7 percent to 34.8 percent. And the proportion of four-year college graduates working in jobs in which the average educational attainment of workers was 14.5 years of school or less, increased from 40.8 percent in 1971 to over half (55.4 percent) in 1995.[12] A substantial share of these changes is due to increased skill requirements in occupations, but the evidence also indicates that some of the growing differences in earnings and occupational options for college graduates reflect downward mobility.

This evidence of downward mobility creates a paradox. It suggests that there is a surplus of college graduates relative to available college-level jobs. But if there is a surplus, why have the wages of college graduates been rising both absolutely and relative to high school graduates since the early 1980s? The mystery is solved by evidence showing that those who are experiencing downward mobility have attained the same educational level but have a considerably lower achievement level, as measured by test scores, than those whose earnings are increasing. In other words, rising wages reflect a scarcity of college graduates with the skills normally associated with a college degree relative to the growing demand for those skills on the job, and downward mobility reflects a growing surplus of low-achieving college graduates.

It appears, then, that the economic returns from postsecondary education depend on what students actually learn as well as where they go to college, what they study, and whether they graduate. For instance, higher grades and test scores are worth an additional 10 percent in earnings among students with the same credentials.[13] Differences in scholastic achievement account for one-third to two-thirds of the earnings gap between whites and African Americans with college degrees. In addition, getting the degree matters; a student who graduates earns twice what a student receives who goes four years and does not bother to get the degree.[14] Moreover, earnings differences related to courses taken and achievement between people at the same educational level, as measured by degrees and years in school, tend to continue over a working lifetime.

THE NEED FOR BETTER INFORMATION

Disparities in the quality of students enrolled in postsecondary education have resulted in a growing differential in the career success of individuals with the same degrees, from the same schools, and in the same programs. But we cannot solve the emerging quality problem in postsecondary education by drumming proprietary schools, remedial programs, and students needing remedial work out of the corps, because the quality problem appears to extend across all two-year and four-year institutions.

Rather than controlling quality by excluding students, we should encourage self-regulation by providing better information to students and their families on readiness, costs, and benefits of further education. Prospective students who find, through diagnostic assessments, that they are not ready for college, that it will take them too long to reach their educational goals, or that the benefits are not worth the time and costs, are unlikely to enroll. Conversely, students who attend college based on realistic expectations of the time and effort required to reach their goals are more likely to stay through graduation.

Anecdotally we know that some people go to college when it will do them little good, and many others don't go because they don't understand the good it will do them. While we don't know the overall effects of better information on encouraging and discouraging enrollment, we can be sure that more informed choices will result in a more effective match between educational resources and individual needs.

A first try toward an outreach-based system is to create measures that reflect the real-world outcomes that can be expected from the choice of curriculum. The traditional measures by which institutions and individuals judge educational attainment—degrees and grades—have their place, but they fall far short of providing current and potential students with the information they need to decide whether to attend college, what courses to take, and when they should leave.

There is ample evidence that the value of a postsecondary education depends on what kind of institution a student attends, whether a student goes to an elite institution, and what curriculum a student takes (engineering majors earn more than English majors, for example). In general, no matter where students go, earnings returns will depend most on what courses they take.

Thus, it makes sense to provide better guidance to students and adults who are considering returning to college about the consequences of their decisions concerning where to go and what curriculum to take. The most consistent and powerful determinants of what students will earn are the curricula they pursue.

Focusing on curricula and the number of courses completed also has the advantage of providing useful guidance to school administrators on how they can improve their programs and can give employers the leverage needed to make constructive changes. In contrast, the alternative of tightening admission standards probably is unpalatable and would not be needed if students had a better idea of the potential returns from attending college.

THE REAL SCHOOL-TO-WORK SYSTEM

Postsecondary education in the United States has become our home-grown school-to-work system. In recent decades, as the economic value of education and training has increased, postsecondary education has expanded to include new vocationally oriented institutional forms, such as community colleges, proprietary schools, and other vocationally oriented institutions.[15]

The natural expansion of the country's existing postsecondary education system to meet new needs has dwarfed attempts to build alternative education and training systems. The postsecondary system represents $210 billion in resources. The federally funded public job training system peaked at $24 billion in 1978 and is currently funded at $7 billion, principally directed at programs under the Job Training Partnership Act (JTPA). Employers spend roughly $64 billion annually and provide training for less than 20 percent of the workforce. Moreover, public job training institutions and employers satisfy a substantial share of their training needs through purchases from higher education institutions.

Our postsecondary system is not only bigger, it is better. Unhappily, our attempts to build a second chance education and training system have taught us that it is the first chance that counts the most. Human capital development is sequential and cumulative. Success is especially difficult for those who can't keep up or who drop out of the mainstream human capital development system, especially when they have taken on family or work responsibilities.

We have learned that the road back into the new economy for those who missed out on their first chance at education and for those who have been dislocated by economic change is routed through the mainstream postsecondary education system and the toll is paid with Pell Grants and student loans.

THE CRITICAL BUT LIMITED ROLE OF EMPLOYERS

In the U.S. system, employers depend on educators to provide skilled entry-level workers.[16] Employers also use educational preparation as the springboard for training on the job, because the highest productivity returns come from training the most highly educated workers. Employer-based training is a critical complement to educational preparation in the U.S. job training system. Employers are second only to schools in preparing people for specific jobs, and they provide or buy most of the job-specific retraining. In addition, employer-sponsored retraining offers the highest productivity returns to companies and the highest earnings returns to individuals.

But we cannot rely on employers to meet all of our new training needs, in spite of the fact that U.S. companies provide the most effective and highest quality job-related training. Market incentives ensure that employer training investments are restrained, incremental, irregular, and skewed in their distribution toward big companies and the best educated workers. Furthermore, employers that train their employees often find them pirated away by firms that do not train but pay higher wages, thereby further discouraging investment in training.[17] Also, U.S. employers, unlike their European counterparts, are unlikely to take on broader educational functions, especially at a time when being lean and flexible are core competitive advantages. As a result, attempts to develop school-to-work apprenticeships, employer training mandates, and work-based skill standards have not taken root in the United States.[18]

TWO CHEERS FOR PUBLIC JOB TRAINING

Currently, low-income students are generally the least likely to obtain education or training on or off the job. Once students fall behind in the first chance education and training system, it is very difficult for them to recover because both successes and failures are reinforcing and cumulative in the education and career system.

Evaluations of programs funded under welfare-to-work and public job training have shown mixed results.[19] In addition, it is especially difficult to make education and training pay off better than even low-wage work or work at lower wages than those earned in a previous job. The least skilled may need years of education and training to move them out of low-wage labor markets. It is far less expensive to move them into a new low-wage job. Dislocated workers often have considerable skills and experience and usually can earn decent wages by quickly returning to work, even if the jobs they get are not as good as the jobs they lost. Thus for both groups the returns from additional schooling must be high enough to offset foregone earnings from currently available jobs.

Dislocated workers make earnings sacrifices to attend school and disadvantaged workers often can use successful work experience as a stepping-stone to better jobs. As a result, job search assistance (JSA) on average has about as large an effect on earnings as training. However, JSA is roughly five times less expensive than training and does not require that a person forego earnings. Thus, evaluations suggest that JSA is the most cost-effective approach, particularly for dislocated workers.[20]

These incentives inherent in the public job training system discourage long-term investments in education and training. As a result, disadvantaged and dislocated clients not only tend to get the wrong kind of help but they also do not get enough of it. The budget of Employment Services, a joint effort of state employment agencies and the U.S. Department of Labor, is sufficient only to provide services costing about $50 per registrant. Furthermore, the disadvantaged and dislocated, especially those with family responsibilities, rarely have access to sufficient income support and family services to pursue an education or training strategy. Even when clients secure education and training in the second chance system, the education and training tend to be short-lived.

It is little wonder that employment and welfare policies currently are dominated by "work first" strategies; the switch was facilitated, in part, by employers' exceptionally strong demand for workers over the past seven years. Work first policies make sense for the most skilled among the unemployed, especially in good economic times. The least educated do not fare well even when jobs are plentiful. The blue-collar economy of the 1950s, when an individual could earn high wages through hard work and loyalty, has gone the way of gold watches at retirement. There are almost 12 million full-time workers who are officially poor and 9.4 million workers who were displaced between 1993 and 1995. The wages of those without some form of postsecondary education have declined to pre-1970s levels and the earnings of high school dropouts have declined to their pre-1960s level. A work first strategy tracks the least-skilled workers into the jobs with the lowest wages, and dislocated workers have to accept lower wages. The current workforce development system does provide a transition from unemployment to work but does not fund sufficient education and training to allow disadvantaged and dislocated workers to make real career progress.

Work first strategies can promote intergenerational mobility but only if employed parents lead to better-educated children. We need to keep in mind that intergenerational mobility now depends principally on more education for children. This was not always so. In the early post-World War II decades, more than two-thirds of upward mobility resulted from robust economic growth that dramatically increased the number of good jobs available. Since the 1970s, growth has been cut in half. We are not creating new good jobs in the volumes we did in the early postwar decades. Since the 1970s, only a third of upward mobility has resulted from economic growth and almost two-thirds from improvements in educational attainment.

THE DISCONNECT BETWEEN WORK AND LEARNING

Although the economic role of postsecondary education is more important than ever, it is not a role that is esteemed highly by educators, because it is viewed, in part, as a role that indulges narrow and superficial commercial interests at the expense of broader and deeper educational purposes. The economic role of postsecondary institutions is often viewed as a Trojan horse inside the gates of the academy, harboring the invasive purposes of the state and the economy.

In an individualistic culture and a political system based on participation, postsecondary education is charged with the responsibility for producing good neighbors and good citizens as well as qualified workers. The inherent conflict between the cultural, political, and economic roles of postsecondary education discourages effective alignment between education and work opportunities. As a result, the relationships between particular educational curricula and job opportunities are not well articulated. The disconnect between work and learning is especially troublesome for nontraditional students because the traditional pace and organization of postsecondary institutions do not fit their complex schedules and life circumstances.

This disconnect is not the fault of educators alone. Education and training are not central to the primary work first mission of public employment and welfare agencies or to the strategic business goals of private employers. Work and learning complement and substitute for each other.

Oftentimes, a job is the best trainer and the most effective way for individuals to achieve economic independence. In other cases, formal learning is preferable to learning on the job because it brings longer-lasting earnings for individuals and more sustained productivity improvements for employers. In general, educators are likely to undervalue the pedagogical or career-enhancing power of learning at work. At the same time, employers and advocates of work-oriented welfare and employment policy do not understand the economic value of formal learning.

The disconnect between employers and education or training institutions creates an information vacuum that makes informed choices difficult. For example, nontraditional students are usually unaware of Pell Grants and student loans until they decide to apply to postsecondary institutions. As a result, student financial aid has little effect on the decisions of low-income students to seek further education.[21] Information, not income, appears to be the principal barrier to access to postsecondary education for these students. Because they are unaware of student aid and long-term earnings returns, the least-advantaged students often choose low-wage jobs over more schooling that eventually would have resulted in a better job.[22]

This lack of information also discourages students from remaining in college and from selecting curricula with the most value in labor markets. Only half of those who enroll receive a postsecondary credential within five years. Furthermore, the growing differential in the wages of college graduates demonstrates that information on the economic returns from different curricula is increasingly important in making educational and career choices.

THE IMPORTANCE OF COUNSELING

The primary impediment to access to college is not tests or money but inadequate information and counseling. First, children need to realize that going to college pays off and that, if they can make the grade, financial aid ensures them of access to college. Moreover, unless we support more—and more effective—counseling, the information we can garner from individual and institutional assessments is likely to go unused. The lack of support for counseling is a problem that begins in elementary and secondary schools. Only 19 states and the District of Columbia mandate that schools provide guidance and counseling services.

Counseling adds value to information; it represents an intermediary service that collects and interprets information on alternative learning and employment choices and likely outcomes. Clients, especially disadvantaged clients with family responsibilities and multiple needs, require advice in making informed choices and customizing educational and career programs to their circumstances. Counseling ensures a sensitivity to clients' ability to benefit from different programs, encouraging program efficiency from the bottom up.

Available data tend to support the need for counseling. Most disadvantaged Americans end up out of school, not because of what they don't do, but because of what they don't know about their alternatives. Research on the characteristics and outcomes of 1992 high school graduates demonstrates the importance of access to college counseling for college enrollment among disadvantaged students. For instance, only about half of 1992 Hispanic high school graduates who were academically qualified to attend a four-year college had enrolled by 1994. However, among those who actually took steps to gain admission, 77 percent had enrolled.[23]

While the enrollment rates of academically qualified Hispanic students were somewhat lower than the enrollment rates of academically qualified students in other race/ethnic groups, the enrollment rates for Hispanic students who were qualified *and followed the prescribed course for admission* to a four-year college were no lower than the enrollment rates of comparable white graduates. The same research also shows that if students from low-income backgrounds take the necessary steps to get to a four-year college, they enroll at the same rates as students from middle-income backgrounds. For academically qualified students, the first step to enrolling in college is engaging in the admission process. Counseling can play a critical role in initiating this process, thereby boosting the rates of actual college enrollment.

INFORMING CHOICES

U.S. postsecondary education and training systems are unique in the number of choices available to a diverse array of students. But choices between work and learning are often not well-informed. Choice encourages high performance but does not guarantee it. Choice without dependable information is guessing, not choosing.

A robust information system answers the question: Education and training for what? The federal government already has access to a significant amount of important job data. Each quarter, private employers report wages, hours worked, and other information for all existing and new jobs to Employment Services. The government uses this information principally to verify eligibility for unemployment insurance and to locate people (e.g., parents who try to avoid child-support payments). Wage records tell us where the jobs are four times every year. Once we know this, it is not hard to predict where the jobs will be and which skills will be necessary to perform them.

Wage records also can be used to evaluate education and training programs. For example, think of the savings that could be captured if these records were searched to determine which training programs resulted in real wage increases and sustained employment and which had no effect. Trainers and educators—and consumers—would know the relative labor-market value of the type of training offered as well as the quality of the training institution. Providers that had poor records would get less business, while successful institutions with good records would attract consumers and grow. This information also could be used to improve the match between job training and available jobs.

In fact, the states of Florida, Texas, and Washington have generated this type of information and have used it to guide funding and program selection, and many other states are in the process of creating such information systems. States are beginning to recognize that clients need to be better informed if they are to choose effectively between school and work and if they are to choose curricula with the highest returns.

THE SOLUTION: AN INFORMATION STRATEGY

The importance of the U.S. postsecondary education system as the primary supplier of career-enhancing skills has grown markedly over the past 25 years. The increased value to both the individual and society of education beyond high school has intensified the problem of providing high-quality learning without restricting access. To economists, this is yet another instance of figuring out how to produce a public good that simultaneously maximizes efficiency and equity.

The obvious danger to the education system is that a failure to adequately control quality will waste a lot of resources and reduce public support for funding postsecondary education. As usual, the brunt of any funding cutbacks will fall on those with the least ability to help themselves: high school graduates from low-income families and individuals needing a second chance because they lost good jobs or never were able to enter the economic mainstream.

Fortunately, we see an equally obvious solution to this problem, at least for those needing a second chance. There is clear evidence that the net returns from postsecondary education are affected to some extent by where students go and to a much greater extent by the number and subject matter of the courses completed, as well as by the ability of individuals to learn while on the job. What appears to have been missing from the workforce development system, including both postsecondary education and job training, is a comprehensive means of helping potential students understand the trade-offs between work and school, and between curricula.

We suggest an information strategy as the best bet for simultaneously maximizing quality, efficiency, and opportunity. With the growth in the importance of postsecondary education and the failure of attempts to create alternatives to the mainstream postsecondary system, it has become clear that postsecondary education in general, and Pell Grants and student loans in particular, are the keystones in the nation's school-to-work system. Yet we have no integrating policy or universally effective performance standards at the interface between postsecondary institutions, labor markets, and employers. The disconnect between postsecondary institutions and labor markets is especially harmful to the least advantaged, who need the most help in making the transition from school to work. Moreover, because of work first mandates and concern about loan defaults and educational quality, we are seeing a simultaneous retreat among educators and employment and welfare policymakers from the use of education and training to assist welfare clients, the unemployed, dislocated workers, and other nontraditional students.

The way forward is to create a new information system. Information is a key asset in integrating fragmented institutional structures and missions while preserving the autonomy of separate organizations. The most important kinds of information required are:

- individual assessments that tell students where they are in their educational progress and what they need to know to achieve their career goals,

- assessments to determine readiness for and placement in academic programs,

- institutional performance measures that show not only outcomes but also the value added to individual knowledge and employability by particular curricula, and

- performance measures that help clients choose between work and training options with full knowledge of the short- and long-term lost opportunity costs and benefits of choosing one option over another.

Dependable information by itself will not suffice in repairing the current disconnect between postsecondary education and labor markets. Intermediaries will be needed to counsel individuals about choices, and a labor exchange will be necessary to provide a common ground where job seekers and employers can find each other.

In the public job training system, the movement toward one-stop career centers is consistent with an information-based approach and holds great promise as a neutral intermediary and labor exchange. The heart of the system is using low-cost public labor exchanges to find work first and then providing high-cost support services as a second chance for clients who cannot find suitable jobs or are particularly likely to benefit from additional education. For individuals who need such additional help, one-stop career centers attempt to:

- assess the sources of the problem, such as poor basic education, lack of vocational skills, lack of child care, or existence of special family circumstances;

- develop an individualized assistance plan by counseling clients about the expected return from different types of financial aid; and

- refer the client to appropriate support services that can provide training as well as counseling, family support, and ongoing evaluation.

Key to the success of one-stop centers is an accurate information base on which those needing a second chance can rely. One type of information is simply knowing what the options are and how to decide between them. Those who need a second chance would have greatly expanded access to counselors, far better technology to obtain information on their own, and the instruction necessary to effectively use information resources.

Another type of information, of at least equal importance, is the information generated by linking wage records to postsecondary participant records. This has proven to be a low-cost means of providing accurate information about the expected returns from school and work. It is precisely this type of information that is needed by counselors and automated information systems so they can do the job of providing clients with information to make informed choices.

The potential benefits of these changes would be enormous. Those most needing help would be able to select the course of action that is most likely to improve their position, without feeling they have been coerced or lack appropriate support from society. Society-at-large would benefit by having a more efficient employment and training system, a better trained workforce, and fewer people in need of direct income support.

Our postsecondary education system would also benefit. First, the central quality versus access trade-off would be resolved by helping individuals make appropriate choices. Second, the total number of people enrolled in some form of postsecondary education would increase substantially, particularly those from lower-middle-income families. The increase would stem from providing better information about the availability of Pell Grants and other forms of aid, which would motivate students to remain enrolled longer.

CONCLUSION

The best evidence suggests that the Pell Grant program has fallen far short of its potential because too many individuals do not know of its existence or are unduly reluctant to apply for aid. At the same time, many individuals leave college too quickly because they underestimate the importance of taking a large variety of courses. Adopting the information strategy advanced here would boost attendance by individuals who currently do not go to college or leave prematurely.

In short, Pell Grants and federal student loans have made training affordable and, thereby, have secured one of the three critical legs of a highly effective second chance education and training system. The key missing components are better information about the career-enhancing returns from postsecondary education and better methods for delivering that information.

ANTHONY P. CARNEVALE *is an authority on education, training, and employment, who currently serves as vice president for public leadership at the Educational Testing Service. His prior career includes service as a presidential appointee as chair of the National Commission for Employment Policy; vice president and director of Human Resource Studies at the Committee for Economic Development; and president of the Institute for Workbased Learning, an applied research center affiliated with the American Society for Training and Development. Carnevale received his B.A. from Colby College and his Ph.D. from the Maxwell School at Syracuse University.*

LOUIS S. JACOBSON *is a labor economist and senior analyst at Westat, Inc. He has pioneered methods to study the effectiveness of community college training programs using unemployment insurance records, and has conducted an assessment of best practices in job matching—a key element in the Department of Labor's Employment Service revitalization project. Jacobson received his Ph.D. in economics from Northwestern University.*

NOTES

1. Among welfare recipients who receive Pell Grants, 55 percent attend community colleges, 25 percent attend four-year institutions, and 20 percent attend proprietary schools. Among dislocated workers who receive Pell Grants, 40 percent attend community colleges, 30 percent attend four-year institutions, and 30 percent attend proprietary schools. The average duration of education or training through a Job Training Partnership Act (JTPA) program—24 weeks for disadvantaged workers and 36 weeks for dislocated workers—is substantially less than the seat time at postsecondary institutions, and the earnings gains of those who attend postsecondary institutions are three times as high as those experienced by welfare clients and dislocated workers trained by public job training programs.
2. Of the 1,165,973 bachelor's degrees conferred in 1993-94, only 20 percent were in cultural studies, literature, liberal arts and sciences, philosophy, religion, history, and the social sciences.
3. The increase in business and professional program enrollment corresponds to a similar increase in the number of business and professional jobs and associated increased earnings relative to other job choices. Business and professional jobs increased as a proportion of total jobs from 30 to 40 percent from 1959 to 1995, and their earnings in these jobs increased from 38 to 50 percent of all earnings. Anthony P. Carnevale and Stephen J. Rose, "Education for What? The New Office Economy" (Princeton, N.J.: Educational Testing Service, forthcoming).
4. Anthony P. Carnevale and Richard A. Fry, *"Generation Y" Goes to College: State College Enrollments, 1995 to 2015* (Princeton, N.J.: Educational Testing Service, forthcoming).

5. John H. Bishop, "Is the Market for College Graduates Headed for a Bust? Demand and Supply Responses to Rising College Wage Premiums," *New England Economic Review* (May/June 1996): 115–35.

6. Carnevale and Fry, forthcoming.

7. U.S. Department of Education, National Center for Education Statistics, *High School and Beyond: Educational Attainment of 1980 High School Sophomores by 1992*, NCES 95-304 (Washington, D.C.: U.S. Government Printing Office, March 1995).

8. In general, the earnings advantages associated with postsecondary education have increased little in absolute terms (except for people with graduate degrees), but the relative differences between people at varying educational levels have increased dramatically. Alternatively, it is not that the college-educated are doing that much better; the fact is, the least-educated are doing that much worse. Moreover, postsecondary education is valuable not only all by itself but also as a bridge to further learning on the job.

9. Malcolm Getz and John J. Siegfried, "Costs and Productivity in American Colleges and Universities," in *Economic Challenges in Higher Education*, 1st ed. (Chicago: University of Chicago Press, 1991).

10. Legislation of the early 1990s sought to reduce defaults under the Guaranteed Student Loan program. Among other initiatives, the legislation required that any school providing undergraduate, nonbaccalaureate degree programs to prepare students for a particular vocation, trade, or career must disclose certain information including: all licensure or certification requirements for the field; the pass rate of the program's graduates on licensure tests or examinations required by the state; job placement rates in the trade students were trained for; and program completion rates. In general, these provisions were put in place to ensure that consumers had accurate information against which to judge the employment claims made by propriety schools in their recruitment efforts; however, many community colleges offered these types of programs and were affected. Furthermore, any institution that makes job placement claims to attract students to enroll must provide this information to remain entitled to Higher Education Act (HEA) Title IV funding. Margot A. Schenet, "Proprietary Schools: The Regulatory Structure" (Washington, D.C.: Congressional Research Service, August 1990).

11. Substantial research indicates that a significant proportion of the increase in the value of a college degree results from the fact that employers no longer trust the quality of a high school education. According to one study, almost half of the increase in the value of four-year credentials is due to employers' loss of faith in high school degrees. Richard J. Murnane and Frank Levy, *Teaching the New Basic Skills* (New York: Free Press, 1996).

12. Daniel Hecker, "Reconciling Conflicting Data on Jobs for College Graduates," *Monthly Labor Review* (July 1992); John Tyler, Richard Murnane, and Frank Levy, "Are College Graduates Really Taking High School Jobs?," *Monthly Labor Review* (December 1995); Frederick L. Pryor and David Schaeffer, "Wages and the University Educated: A Paradox Resolved," *Monthly Labor Review* (July 1997).

13. People with four-year degrees earn twice as much as those with two-year degrees. Variations in majors among those with a baccalaureate degree can create as much as a 50 percent difference in starting salaries, which can result in a 100 percent difference by the time students are 45 to 64 years of age. U.S. Department of Education, National Center for Education Statistics, *The Condition of Education,* NCES 97-388 (Washington, D.C.: U.S. Government Printing Office, June 1997); Daniel Hecker, "Earnings of College Graduates, 1993," *Monthly Labor Review* (December 1995).

14. David A. Jaegar and Marianne Page, "Degrees Matter: New Evidence on Sheepskin Effects in the Returns to Education," *Review of Economics and Statistics* (November 1996).

15. Anthony P. Carnevale, Donna M. Desrochers, and Richard A. Fry, "Investing in Education and Training for Higher Growth," in *The Rising Tide,* ed. Jerry Jasinowski (New York: John Wiley, 1997).

16. In the United States, formal education is the bedrock investment in human capital; its volume far exceeds formal training on the job, even when estimates of informal learning on the job are included. We invest $510 billion in formal education compared with $64 billion in formal employer-provided training and perhaps double that if informal learning on the job is included. Historically about 27 percent of productivity growth has relied on increased educational attainment, mostly due to increased high school graduation rates. As these rates approach 90 percent, future productivity returns from formal education will have to come from quality improvements in elementary/secondary education and improvements in access, retention, and quality in higher education.

17. Anthony P. Carnevale and Donna M. Desrochers, "The High Road, the Low Road and the Muddy Middle Path," Issue paper for the Economic Policy Institute Conference on Restoring Broadly Shared Prosperity (1997).

18. In the future, employers may need to rely on the postsecondary system for even more of their job training requirements as they attempt to close the emerging training gap on the job. Demand for job training has increased since the early 1980s and employers are having trouble keeping up. They have responded by increasing their own training efforts and by increasing the amount of education and training they buy outside, principally from postsecondary institutions, but future employer training needs are even more daunting. As the workforce shifts toward managerial, professional, and technical workers who require more training on the job, employers will have to make an additional annual investment of $15 billion by 2005, over and above the $64 billion already spent annually, just to maintain current training levels, and they will have to spend an additional $80 billion to extend employer-sponsored training to half of their workers. Carnevale and Desrochers, 1997.

19. "Training" sponsored by JTPA includes a wide variety of programs such as high school vocational education, proprietary schools, apprenticeships, vocational rehabilitation, and others. Training as defined by JTPA includes informal on-the-job training and work experience. Returns from training sponsored

through the JTPA tend to increase earnings by 5 percent to 7 percent over two and a half years, while each full year of college increases future earnings by a full 10 percent.

20. Louis S. Jacobson, "Compensatory Programs," in *Imports, Exports, and the American Worker,* ed. Susan Collins (Washington, D.C.: Brookings Institution Press, forthcoming).

21. Thomas J. Kane, "Rising Public College Tuition and College Entry: How Well Do Public Subsidies Promote Access to College?" NBER Working Paper No. 5164 (July 1995).

22. U.S. Department of Education, National Center for Education Statistics, *Access to Postsecondary Education for the 1992 High School Graduates,* NCES 98-105 (Washington, D.C.: U.S. Government Printing Office, October 1997); Council of Economic Advisers, "Investing in Education and Training," Chapter 7 in the *Economic Report of the President* (Washington, D.C.: U.S. Government Printing Office, 1996).

23. U.S. Department of Education, *Access to Postsecondary Education,* 1997.

1997: THE TWENTY-FIFTH ANNIVERSARY PELL GRANT CONFERENCE

© MARTY LaVOR

During the opening session of the Twenty-Fifth Anniversary Pell Grant Conference in the House Education Committee hearing room, former Senator Pell was greeted with a spirited ovation by the 200 in attendance. To the senator's right is his wife, Nuala Pell. Seated is former Rep. Gus Hawkins (D-CA), who chaired the House Education and Labor Committee from 1984 to 1991. Standing at right is Ann Coles of The Education Resources Institute.

© MARTY LaVOR

At center, Pell Grant Twenty-Fifth Anniversary Conference presenters Sam Kipp and Mike McPherson at the opening session, "Memory."

© MARTY LaVOR

Bob Shireman, White House senior policy advisor, discusses the administration's current proposals for higher education.

© MARTY LaVOR

Walter Moulton, director of financial aid at Bowdoin College, urges restoring the federal/state/institutional partnership to ensure that the greatest benefit goes to those with the greatest need.

David Evans visits with his former boss, Senator Pell, as former Rep. Hawkins looks on.

© MARTY LAVOR

Humphrey Doermann from Macalester College reminds the conference attendees of the federal government's primary commitment to providing access for students from low-income families.

© MARTY LAVOR

Arnold Mitchem, executive director of the National Council of Educational Opportunity Associations, underscores the need to "tie dollars to aspirations."

Left to right, former U.S. Department of Education official, John Phillips, former congressional staff aide, Tom Wolanin, and Lois Rice of the Brookings Institution.

© MARTY LAVOR

© MARTY LAVOR

Left to right, former congressional staff aide Rick Jerue, former Representative Pat Williams (D-MT), who served as master of ceremonies for the Pell Grant Twenty-Fifth Anniversary dinner celebration, and Larry Gladieux of the College Board.

At the gala dinner, Senator James Jeffords (R-VT) hails Senator Pell's long-standing commitment to access to higher education for all Americans.

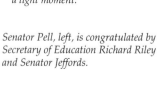

After regaling the crowd with amusing anecdotes of working with Senator Pell, former Senator Tom Eagleton (D-MO) and Senator Chris Dodd (D-CT) share a light moment.

Senator Pell, left, is congratulated by Secretary of Education Richard Riley and Senator Jeffords.

*Rep. Chaka Fattah (D-PA),
a former Pell Grant recipient, discusses
his proposed 21st Century Scholars
Program that would provide mentoring
and early notice of Pell Grants and
other college aid to low-income sixth-
grade students.*

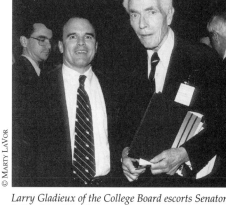

*Larry Gladieux of the College Board escorts Senator
Pell to his table of honor at the evening reception.*

*Lois Rice of the Brookings Institution
celebrates the Pell Grant's success with
former Senator Eagleton and
College Board President
Donald M. Stewart.*

*Senator Pell is thanked by four recipients of the grant that bears his name. Left
to right: Anthony Samu, Angela Neal, Nathan Ambrose, and Eileen Withey.*

Imagination

We have focused to this point on the origins and outcomes of the Pell Grant program. What about needs and prospects for the next 25 years?

One thing is clear as we head into the next century: Higher education is more important than ever—to our economy and competitive position in the world, to an individual's chances of sharing in American prosperity, and to narrowing the gaps between rich and poor. It is also clear that demographic trends will pose enormous challenges to the country and higher education. There will be a greater need than ever for Pell Grants and related support aimed at helping more of the coming generation to prepare for and succeed in some form of postsecondary education.

In "Imagination," our authors consider the challenges of the coming century, and ideas for strengthening public policy to meet those challenges.

Demographic Trends and Their Impact on the Future of the Pell Grant Program

Samuel M. Kipp III

Abstract. *By the year 2010 the number of 18- to 24-year-olds will rise by five million. While the potential pool of high school graduates and college students will increase substantially, the only thing that will be traditional about this growing cohort will be its age. It will be even more ethnically diverse than the general population, and the most rapid growth will occur among groups traditionally more likely to drop out of school, less likely to enroll in college preparatory course work, less likely to graduate from high school, less likely to enroll in college, and least likely to persist to earn a baccalaureate degree. Given the changing composition of the college-age population, the high proportion of African Americans and Hispanics with low incomes, and the current course-taking and high school graduation patterns among these same groups, dramatic steps will be needed just to keep overall college participation rates from falling. The future is hardly on automatic pilot, and success will require major investments in Pell Grants and other financial aid, along with greatly improved academic preparation, to sustain or improve current participation levels.*

We live in a world revolutionized by the creation of a truly global economy. Economist Lester Thurow speaks of a fundamental "technology shift to an era dominated by man-made, brainpower industries that have no predetermined homes and could be located anywhere people are able to create, mobilize and organize the necessary brainpower."[1] This shift has profound implications for economic development, economic well-being, and the role of education at both the K-12 and postsecondary levels. The nation's colleges and universities educate almost 12.2 million undergraduate students. Today, 6 out of every 10 high school graduates enroll in college during the year following their graduation. The extraordinary demand for highly educated and highly skilled workers places a tremendous premium on the acquisition of advanced education and training. In 1995, the average male in his late twenties or early thirties with a baccalaureate degree earned over 55 percent more, and female bachelor's degree recipients earned nearly 75 percent more, than their counterparts with only a high school diploma. Those without education and training beyond high school are being left behind. Indeed, most of the earnings gap was a result of the sharp 29 percent decline in real terms in the median income of male high school graduates and the plummeting real incomes of high school dropouts.

Safeguarding and extending educational opportunity has become a vital concern to both individuals and the larger society. The nation's capacity and commitment to do so will be seriously tested in the decades ahead. This paper examines demographic trends, earnings patterns, and changes in family and household structure. It also analyzes trends in high school completion, preparation for college, and academic performance—particularly for low-income and minority students. The focus is on the interaction of these trends, their likely impact on future undergraduate enrollment, and their implications for the Pell Grant program.

PROJECTED GROWTH OF THE POPULATION

The Census Bureau projects that between 1995 and 2010 the nation's population will increase by 35 million people, or 13 percent, from 263 million to 298 million. As Figure 1 shows, however, growth will vary tremendously by region, with 82 percent of all the population growth in the country over the next 15 years occurring in the South and West. The largest states in the Northeast—Connecticut, Massachusetts, New Jersey, New York, and Pennsylvania—are expected to experience continued heavy out-migration. And most of their domestic net migration losses are not expected to be offset by gains from foreign immigration.

The Midwest, too, will experience sluggish growth, adding only 4 million people to its current 62 million and growing at only half the national rate. Again, net domestic migration losses, particularly in Illinois, Michigan, and Ohio, will be the major factor.

The South will add about 16 million people to its present base of 92 million, an increase of 17 percent, largely through a surplus of births over deaths and substantial gains from domestic migration. Only Florida, Texas, and Virginia are expected to have sizable gains from foreign immigration as well.

The West's population of almost 58 million will grow by 13 million, or 22 percent. Anticipated net domestic migration losses in California have

FIGURE 1.   *Population Growth Rates by Region, 1995 to 2010*

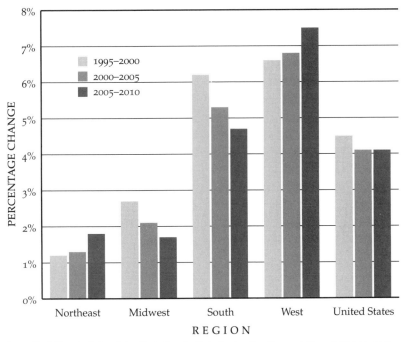

Source: Paul Campbell, *Population Projections for States by Age, Sex, Race, and Hispanic Origin: 1995-2025*, (Washington, D.C.: U.S. Census Bureau, October 1996).

slowed since the recession-wracked early-1990s, but will continue to fuel growth in most neighboring states. California's own growth will stem from a net natural increase and the arrival of an anticipated 290,000 additional foreign immigrants each year—34 percent of the nation's new immigrants.[2]

AGE STRUCTURE OF THE POPULATION

The age distribution of the population will change in ways that will have a major impact on the potential growth of enrollment in higher education (see Table 1).

The 18-to-24-year-old cohort will grow rapidly. The size of this group, which makes up 63 percent of all undergraduates and over 82 percent of full-time undergraduates, will increase by over five million, or 21 percent, by 2010. This group will grow by just 5 percent nationally over the

TABLE 1. *Changes in the Size of Key Age Groups, 1995 to 2010*

Age Group	1995 Population	Percentage of Total Population	2010 Population	Percentage of Total Population	Increase	Percentage Increase
18- and 19-year-olds	7,050	2.7%	9,004	3.0%	1,954	27.7%
20- to 24-year-olds	17,882	6.8	21,134	7.1	3,252	18.2
25- to 34-year-olds	40,873	15.6	38,292	12.9	-2,581	-6.3
35- to 54-year-olds	73,547	28.0	82,085	27.6	8,538	11.6
65 years and over	33,532	12.8	39,408	13.2	5,876	17.5

Source: Paul Campbell, *Population Projections for States by Age, Sex, Race, and Hispanic Origin: 1995–2025*, (Washington, D.C.: U.S. Census Bureau, October 1996), 74, 80.
Note: Population figures in thousands.

remaining years of this century, and nine states will actually have fewer 18- to 24-year-olds in the year 2000 than they had in 1995. But between 2000 and 2010, the 18-to-24-year-old cohort will increase by 15 percent, the strongest growth in nearly three decades (see Table 1).

In contrast, the 25-to-34-year-old cohort will decline. The size of this group, currently the source of almost one-third of all part-time undergraduates and nearly half of all graduate and first-professional students, will shrink by about three million, or 6 percent, by 2010. Nearly half of that loss will occur in New England and the Mid-Atlantic regions, one-fourth will be in the Midwest, and the remainder in the South. Only Texas and the states in the West, except for California, will experience significant growth in their 25-to-34-year-old populations.

Older age cohorts will grow. The 35-to-54-year-old group, now the source of nearly one-third of all part-time undergraduates and nearly half of all part-time graduate students, will grow by almost 12 percent in the next 15 years. But the size of the younger half of this cohort will begin to decline after the turn of the century, while the most rapid increase will occur among the baby boomers in the 45-to-54-year-old range. The country's 65-and-older population will grow by almost six million, or nearly 18 percent.

INCREASING NUMBER OF HIGH SCHOOL GRADUATES

These shifts in the age composition of the population are significant for higher education because of substantial differences in the college participation rates of the different age groups, as shown in Table 2.

TABLE 2. *1995 College Enrollment by Age Group, Attendance Pattern, and Degree Level*

Age Group	Undergraduate		Graduate		First-Professional	
	Full-Time	Part-Time	Full-Time	Part-Time	Full-Time	Part-Time
18 and 19	36.2%	11.3%	0.0%	0.0%	0.0%	0.0%
20 to 24	45.5	26.1	26.3	9.3	42.4	9.1
25 to 34	12.0	31.4	52.3	43.9	48.3	54.3
35 and over	6.3	31.1	22.0	48.5	9.3	36.0
Total	**58.4**	**41.6**	**41.4**	**59.6**	**89.5**	**10.5**

Source: U.S. Department of Education, NCES, *Digest of Education Statistics 1996,* (Washington, D.C.: U.S. Government Printing Office, 1996).

Note: Total shows the percentage of students at that level who are full- or part-time. Other figures are the percentage of students in that degree level and credit-load category in a particular age group.

Furthermore, the wide regional disparities in the growth rates of key age groups mean that enrollment demand will be extraordinarily strong for colleges and universities in some states in the West and South and quite weak in others, particularly in the Northeast, Midwest, and Great Plains regions.

Unlike the 1980s and early 1990s, when the number of recent high school graduates plunged by 700,000 (24 percent), that number is expected to increase by more than 25 percent over the next 10 years. In 1998, the Western Interstate Commission for Higher Education (WICHE) and the College Board projected that growth patterns will vary widely from state to state. Six states plus the District of Columbia are expected to have fewer high school graduates in 2011 than in 1995. However, 16 states will have increases in excess of 25 percent, with Nevada projected to more than double the size of its graduating class. These large-scale increases are taking place, for the most part, in the Pacific, Southern, and Atlantic border areas, what is referred to as the "crescent." The midwestern and northern states, alternatively, are projected to have moderate or no increases.[3]

DRAMATIC CHANGES IN ETHNIC COMPOSITION

While the pool of high school graduates and potential college students will increase substantially, the only thing traditional about this growing cohort will be its age. Three-fourths of the future population growth will be among racial and ethnic minorities (see Table 3).

TABLE 3.   *Population Growth Among Racial/Ethnic Groups, 1995 to 2010*

Racial/Ethnic Group	1995 Population	Percentage	2010 Population	Percentage	Number Increase	Percentage Increase	Percentage of Total Increase
Non-Hispanic white	193,523	73.7%	202,390	68.0%	8,867	4.6%	25.4%
Non-Hispanic African American	31,591	12.0	37,466	12.6	5,875	18.6	16.8
Asian	8,779	3.3	14,402	4.8	5,623	64.1	16.1
American Indian	1,930	0.7	2,321	0.8	391	20.2	1.1
Hispanic	26,932	10.2	41,138	13.8	14,206	52.7	40.6
Total	**262,755**	**100.0**	**297,716**	**100.0**	**34,961**	**13.3**	**100.0**

Source: Paul Campbell, *Population Projections for States by Age, Sex, Race, and Hispanic Origin: 1995–2025* (Washington, D.C.: U.S. Census Bureau, October 1996), 61, 67.
Note: Population figures in thousands.

The non-Hispanic white population will increase slightly, but will decline in relative terms from 74 percent of the total U.S. population in 1995 to 68 percent in 2010. In New England and the Mid-Atlantic regions, this population will actually decline in both relative and absolute terms.[4]

The Asian population will increase by 64 percent and will account for nearly one-sixth of total U.S. growth—over five and one-half million of the 35 million. This population is becoming much more heterogeneous, with the most rapid growth occurring among Vietnamese, Cambodians, other Southeast Asians, and Filipinos. Over half of the Asian population growth—three million—will occur in the West, and almost two and one-half million of that will be in California and Washington.

Hispanics will account for an extraordinary 41 percent of the country's total population growth in the next 15 years. The Hispanic population will increase rapidly in percentage terms in most states, but growth will be concentrated most heavily in fewer than 10 states. More than 35 percent of this population increase will be in California alone, and nearly half will be in the West (see Figure 2). An additional 15 percent will occur in two other states: Texas and Florida. Except for Illinois, Florida, and Texas, Hispanics will not have an appreciable presence in the Midwest or the South. By 2010, the states with the largest proportion of Hispanics in their total population will be New Mexico (42 percent), California (38 percent), Texas (32 percent), Arizona (26 percent), Nevada (19 percent), Florida (19 percent), New York (18 percent), and Colorado (17 percent).

FIGURE 2. *Ethnic Composition of the Population by Region, 1995 and 2010*

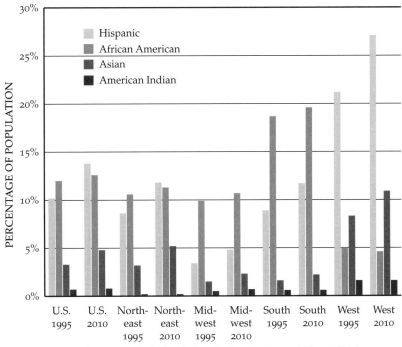

Source: Paul Campbell, *Population Projections for States by Age, Sex, Race, and Hispanic Origin: 1995–2025* (Washington, D.C.: U.S. Census Bureau, October 1996), 61, 67.

Two-thirds of the increase among the non-Hispanic African-American population will occur in the South. Whereas African Americans will account for over one-sixth of the nation's total population growth, they will account for one-fourth of the growth in the South. Outside the South, just six states will experience increases of 150,000 or more—California, Illinois, Michigan, New Jersey, New York, and Ohio.

Of particular importance to educators is the fact that the nation's school-age population is even more ethnically diverse than the general population. This reflects differential birth rates and migration patterns. For example, Hispanic youth in the 18-to-24-year-old cohort made up 13 percent of that cohort in 1995 and will account for 17 percent in 2010, compared with 10 percent and 14 percent of the overall population in those two years. African-American youth in the same age range account-ed for 14 percent of 18-to-24-year-olds in 1995 and will make up over 14 percent in 2010, compared with 12 percent and nearly 13 percent of the overall population.[5] With the exception of Asians, the most rapid population growth is occurring among groups that traditionally have been more likely to drop out of school and less likely to enroll in college preparatory course work, graduate from high school, enroll in college, and persist to earn a baccalaureate degree.

NATIONAL PROJECTIONS OF COLLEGE ENROLLMENT

Projections of future undergraduate enrollment are robust but changing. Four years ago, the National Center for Education Statistics (NCES) projected that 940,000 more undergraduate students would enroll in 2005 than the 13 million it anticipated in 1995. NCES based these projected increases on a number of factors: the expected growth in the number of high school graduates, other demographic trends, the impressive enrollment growth in the late-1980s and early-1990s despite the shrinking size of the pool of traditional college-age students, and improved college participation rates among the traditional college-age cohort. Actual undergraduate enrollment in 1995, however, was 12.2 million, or 800,000 fewer than expected. This error in projecting reminds us of the dangers inherent in assuming current trends will continue. It is all too easy to miss key turning points or underestimate the significance of exceptions to seemingly dominant patterns.

Nonetheless, in 1996 NCES projected that undergraduate enrollment would still reach 14 million in 2005, an increase of 1.8 million students. This revised forecast was based on actual 1995 enrollment levels and the assumption that participation rates would rebound quickly from recession levels and then increase an additional 10 percent for 18- to 19-year-olds and 5 percent for 20- to 24-year-olds.[6]

Until recently, NCES forecasts, along with equally robust enrollment projections for a number of rapidly growing western and southern states, reflected a widely shared consensus about the looming impact of a "baby boom echo" on future demand for higher education. Yet the predicted growth has yet to materialize in many of the high population-growth states.[7] Some state planners, legislators, and higher education officials seem surprised enrollment has not yet matched expectations. Others insist that the anticipated boom in demand, which has been referred to as "Tidal Wave II," is still coming but concede that enrollment forecasting has become trickier.

In its 1997 and 1998 forecasts, NCES revised its projection of future undergraduate enrollment levels sharply downward. Table 4 compares the four NCES forecasts and an alternative by this author. NCES now expects nearly one-half million fewer undergraduates to enroll in 2000 than it previously predicted. It also forecasts that 400,000 to 500,000 fewer undergraduates will enroll in 2005 than the 14 million it estimated in its 1995 and 1996 projections. According to NCES, full-time enrollment is still expected to grow faster than part-time and four-year college enrollment faster than two-year nationally. This author's own projection shows a slightly smaller growth rate overall than the most recent NCES forecasts.

TABLE 4. *Actual and Projected Undergraduate Enrollment, 1995 to 2010*

Year	Actual 1995	Projected 2000	Projected 2005	Projected 2006	Projected 2007	Projected 2010
NCES 1995	13,029.0*	13,411.0	13,969.0			
NCES 1996	12,231.7	13,336.0	14,045.0	14,189.0		14,789.0**
NCES 1997	12,231.7	12,832.0	13,647.0	13,822.0	14,017.0	14,590.0**
NCES 1998	12,231.7	12,915.0	13,511.0	13,685.0	13,850.0	14,393.0**
Kipp 1996	12,231.7	12,771.3	13,452.2			14,272.7

*Enrollment figures are in thousands. The NCES 1995 undergraduate enrollment projection proved to be 797,300 students higher than actual enrollment.
**NCES 1996, 1997, and 1998 do not yet go out to 2010 so the figures shown here are a rough extrapolation. Kipp forecasts are based on 1995 age-specific participation rates and U.S. Census Bureau forecasts of the size of the 18- and 19-year-old, 20-to-24-year-old, 25-to-34-year-old, and 35-to-54-year-old populations in 2000, 2005, and 2010.

There are at least five reasons why actual future enrollment growth may not be as robust as some have predicted. Most forecasts assume:

- Student preparation for college will improve, but the record so far is mixed at best, especially for low-income and minority students.

- Overall participation rates will increase, but even holding them steady could prove difficult to achieve.

- Institutions of higher education will have the physical capacity to accommodate more students on campus or through distance learning, but there is a geographic mismatch between available space and the states with the greatest potential for increased enrollment.

- The rate of increase in college costs will not be an obstacle, but it has slowed only slightly and more than two decades of rapidly rising costs could affect decisions about whether and where to enroll.

- College will remain affordable and sufficient financial aid will be available, but the potential pool of future college students is likely to be considerably less affluent and thus less able to afford rising college costs than current students.

HIGH SCHOOL GRADUATION AND STUDENT
PREPARATION FOR COLLEGE

K-12 schooling is improving only slowly and time is running out for many in the next cohort of potential college students. *Education Week* and the Pew Foundation concluded in a sobering report, *Quality Counts 1996: The State of the States,* "Public education systems in the 50 states are riddled with excellence and rife with mediocrity. Despite 15 years of earnest efforts to improve public schools and raise student achievement states haven't made much progress." More significant, in light of the growing ethnic diversity of the school-age population and the projection of even greater diversity in the next 15 years, the report found that "the quality of a child's education depends greatly on skin color, family income, and where he or she lives . . . . We have constructed an educational system so full of inequities that it actually exacerbates the challenges of race and poverty, rather than ameliorates them. Simply put, we take students who have less to begin with and give them less in school, too."[8] If these patterns endure, they will prove to be a formula for educational, economic, and social disaster.

In 1995, four million, or 12 percent of all 16- to 24-year-olds who had left school had not received a high school diploma. Dropout rates vary widely depending on the socioeconomic status of students and their ethnic background (see Figure 3). Young adults from families with the lowest incomes were eight times more likely to drop out than those from families with high incomes, a pattern that has changed little over the past 20 years. And while the gap between African-American and white dropout rates has closed somewhat (a 3.5 percentage point gap compared to 10 or 11 percentage points two decades earlier), the substantial gap between Hispanics and the other groups has not closed (30 percent compared with 12 percent for African Americans and 9 percent for whites). Furthermore, 56 percent of young Hispanics who have not completed high school have not progressed past the ninth grade. This compares with 31 percent of white and 27 percent of African-American dropouts.[9]

Dropout rates in the South (14 percent) and West (15 percent), where the percentage of African-American and Hispanic students is highest, were at least one and one-half times those in the Northeast (8 percent) and Midwest (9 percent). The white dropout rate in the South was also much higher than for whites in any other region.[10]

The large number of Hispanic noncompleters includes young immigrants without a high school diploma or GED who did not enroll in school after immigrating to this country. The dropout rate for Hispanic immigrants aged 16 to 24 was over 46 percent while the comparable rate among those born in this country was 18 percent. This is in marked contrast with historical patterns and with those for other more recent immigrant groups. In fact, among all other ethnic/racial groups, the dropout rate for foreign-born immigrants has generally been lower than for native-born students.

Anticipated increases in the number of high school graduates are predicated on an increase in the number of 17- and 18-year-olds and in the

FIGURE 3. *Dropout Rates of 16- to 24-Year-Olds by Income and Ethnicity, 1995*

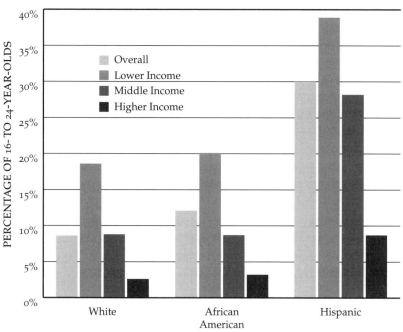

Source: U.S. Department of Education, NCES, *Digest of Education Statistics 1996* (Washington, D.C.: U.S. Government Printing Office, 1996).

percentage who will graduate by 2005. The substantially lower high school completion rates among Hispanics and their growing proportion of the overall 17- and 18-year-old population, especially in the West, make any increase in overall completion rates unlikely. Asians, the fastest growing ethnic group, have above-average completion rates, but the size of the Asian high school cohort is not large enough to offset the Hispanic impact on overall rates. Indeed, had the 18-to-24-year-old population in 1995 had the ethnic composition it will have in 2010, there would have been 2 percent, or 370,000, fewer high school graduates in this cohort.

The overall percentage of students completing high school has remained fairly stable since 1990, but this stability is deceiving because the rate for those graduating from high school on time with a regular diploma has actually declined, from 81 to 78 percent. At the same time, the proportion receiving a GED has increased from less than 5 percent to more than 7 percent. The percentage receiving a GED or completing high school by other means has increased by 2.3 percentage points for whites, 3.3 percentage points for African Americans, and 6 percentage points for Hispanics.[11]

While the notable improvement in the percentage of 18-to-24-year-olds completing high school through the GED and other programs is encouraging, especially for Hispanic youth, the impact on future college enrollment will probably be minimal. Data from the National Education Longitudinal Study confirm that of those who fail to complete high school through regular diploma programs or who do so by securing a GED, few subsequently enroll in postsecondary education. Less than 10 percent of the 1988 eighth graders who later dropped out and less than one-third who went on to become GED recipients enrolled in postsecondary education by fall 1994. Most of those who did attended proprietary schools or community colleges and generally enrolled in certificate or nondegree programs.[12]

COURSE-TAKING PATTERNS AND COLLEGE ENROLLMENT

There is abundant evidence that the preparation and performance of high school students who take college admission tests has improved somewhat over the past decade. More of these seniors are taking honors courses, more are taking courses essential for strong preparation for college, and more are earning advanced placement credits.[13] These test takers, however, represent only about 60 percent of high school seniors, and most of them are from middle- or upper-income families and are planning to attend four-year colleges and universities. For many other high school students, the trends are hardly encouraging, especially for those from lower-income families and those who are African American or Hispanic.

Between 1982 and 1992, the proportion of lower-income students taking college preparatory courses in high school increased from 20 to 23 percent. Yet students from middle-income families were still nearly twice as likely as those from lower-income families to enroll in such courses, and those from upper-income families were nearly three times more likely to do so. By ethnic group, only 35 percent of African-American and just 30 percent of Hispanic students enroll in college preparatory courses in high school, compared with 51 percent of Asians and 45 percent of non-Hispanic whites.[14]

While the sharp reduction in high school vocational training and the increase in the number of students taking general education courses may appear to reflect a democratizing trend, it is not clear that this curricular shift is serving most students well. Fewer than half of all high school students—but more than two-thirds of those who drop out—are enrolled in general studies programs. Moreover, these less challenging and often poorly focused general studies programs leave many of those who do not graduate and go on to college with few marketable job skills.

Table 5 shows the rates at which white, African-American, and Hispanic 18- to 24-year-olds enroll in postsecondary education. Access has increased

TABLE 5. *Enrollment Rates of 18- to 24-Year-Olds by Race/Ethnicity, 1980 and 1995*

College Enrollment Rates	White	African American	Hispanic	Total
1980: All 18- to 24-year-olds	27.3%	19.4%	16.1%	25.7%
1995: All 18- to 24-year-olds	37.9	27.5	20.7	34.3
1980: 18-to-24-year-old high school graduates	31.0	26.0	27.6	30.5
1995: 18-to-24-year-old high school graduates	44.0	35.4	35.2	42.3
1980: High school graduates enrolling within one year	49.9	41.8	49.9	49.3
1995: High school graduates enrolling within one year	62.6	51.4	53.8	61.9

Source: U.S. Department of Education, NCES, *Digest of Education Statistics 1996,* Tables 179 and 182.
Note: These college enrollment rates probably are overstated because they are based on the civilian, noninstitutional population, not the total 18-to-24-year-old population. Furthermore, for these computations NCES assumed that all those enrolled in college were high school graduates.

for all groups since 1980, but large gaps remain. The college enrollment rates of African Americans and Hispanics are still considerably lower than those of whites. Many factors create and sustain these disparities, including the patterns of poor schooling and preparation described above. Significant economic barriers also have an impact.

RISING COLLEGE COSTS

In 1980, both tuition and the total cost of college attendance began to increase faster than the rate of inflation (see Table 6). In constant 1995 dollars, undergraduate tuition increased by over 52 percent at public universities in the 1980s, or four times as fast as the increase in expenditures per full-time equivalent (FTE) student. At private universities, tuition increased by 72 percent, or nearly triple the rate of increase in expenditures per FTE. In the first half of the 1990s, tuition increased an additional 27 percent at public institutions and 19 percent at private. The average tuition at public two-year colleges increased less in dollar amount than at four-year institutions, but still rose 78 percent between 1980 and 1995. The overall cost of attendance increased by 54 percent at public universities and by 93 percent at private universities between 1980 and 1995.[15]

STAGNANT AND INCREASINGLY UNEQUAL FAMILY INCOMES

For many undergraduates, the impact of rising college costs has been compounded by simultaneous changes in individual and family incomes. The median income for 25-to-34-year-old males began to decline in real terms after 1973. That decline accelerated after 1980, particularly for young males with only a high school diploma. Median income for 35-to-44-year-old males followed suit after 1980 and for males in the 45-to-54-year-old cohort it was flat from 1980 to 1995. Had it not been for the increased participation of women in the labor force during the late 1970s and 1980s, average family incomes would not have continued increasing as they did until 1990.[16]

The experiences of families from 1980 to 1995 varied considerably depending on age, education, and general economic position. The median and average incomes of families whose heads were 45 to 54 years

TABLE 6. *Average Tuition and Total Cost of Attendance at Public and Private Institutions, 1980-81 to 1995-96 (constant 1995 dollars)*

College Type and Cost	1980	1985	1990	1995	Change 1980-95
Public two-year college tuition	$ 688	$ 898	$ 937	$ 1,228	+78.5%
Public university tuition	1,609	2,152	2,455	3,107	+93.0
Public university cost of attendance	4,770	5,809	6,350	7,347	+54.0
Private university tuition	7,520	10,331	12,938	15,363	+104.3
Private university cost of attendance	11,555	15,459	18,764	22,155	+91.7

Source: NCES, *Digest*, Table 309.

old—those most likely to have children of college age—increased steadily in real terms throughout this period. However, growth in average incomes was more rapid than in median incomes after 1980, indicating that family income growth was uneven. Those in the upper two quintiles enjoyed a substantial and widening advantage over the 60 percent of families below them on the income scale. Average income for families in the 45-to-54-year-old cohort was 11 percent above the median in 1980, 16 percent above by 1990, and 21 percent above by 1995.[17]

Median household income also varied significantly by race and ethnicity. Overall, median household income was $32,264 in 1995 and less than 12 percent of all households had incomes that put them below the federal poverty level. Median white household income was $35,126 and 7 percent of these households lived in poverty, while among African-American and Hispanic households, the median incomes were $21,027 and $23,421, respectively, or over one-third less than for whites. And more than 27 percent of these minority households lived in poverty, four times the percentage for white households.

Household incomes and the incidence of poverty varied even more depending on family structure. In 1995, median household income for married-couple households was $45,041 and only 6 percent of all such households lived in poverty. In contrast, the median income for single-parent families headed by a female was only $19,872. Part of the explanation for this striking disparity in income was that single-parent families do not have a second wage earner. Among married-couple families with children under 18, 91 percent of the fathers and 67 percent of the mothers were employed.[18] Single-parent families headed by a female now account for nearly 14 percent of white households, almost one-fourth of Hispanic households, and almost half of African-American households. In addition, more than one out of three single-parent families live in poverty.[19]

COLLEGE COSTS AND ABILITY TO PAY

Table 7 shows the rising share of family income represented by tuition and cost of college attendance from 1980 to 1995. In 1980, the average total cost of attending a public university was equivalent to 10 percent of the median income of families whose heads were 45 to 54 years old. At private universities, the average total cost was equivalent to 24 percent. By 1990, however, the steady increase in college costs outpaced the growth in median family income, and the total cost of attendance at public and private universities, respectively, was now equivalent to 12 and 35 percent of median income. These trends continued through the first half of the 1990s except that tuition increased faster at public institutions than at private ones. By 1995, the average cost of attendance at public and private universities, respectively, rose to 14 and 41 percent of median family income.[20]

Obviously, not all families have been similarly affected by rising college costs. For the lowest 60 percent of families in the income distribution, tuition and total cost of attendance were equivalent to a much more substantial proportion of their income than for the average family even in 1980. But the stagnant to deteriorating income levels for such families since then have exacerbated the effects of rising college costs. By 1995, the average cost of attendance at a public university, before factoring in financial aid, represented the equivalent of 40 percent of income for families in the lowest-income quintile, or three times as large a proportion of income as for median-income families. At private institutions, the before-aid cost of attendance amounted to well over 100 percent of the income of the least affluent families.

Sandy Baum has cautioned, appropriately, that a college education is a long-term investment, not a consumption good to be paid for out of current income. Clearly, paying the cost of attending a public university out of current income is out of the question for most families in the lower range of the income distribution. At private universities, it is out

TABLE 7.   *College Costs as a Percentage of Median Family Income for Families Whose Heads Were 45 to 54 Years of Age, 1980 to 1995*

College Type and Cost	1980	1985	1990	1995	Change 1980-95
Public university tuition	3.4%	4.2%	4.6%	5.7%	+2.3%
Public university cost of attendance	9.9	11.3	11.8	13.5	+3.6
Private university tuition	15.7	20.1	24.1	28.3	+12.6
Private university cost of attendance	24.1	30.1	35.0	40.8	+16.7

Source: NCES, *Digest,* Table 309; Census Bureau, *Historical Income Tables—Families,* Table F-11, "Age of Householder—Families by Median and Mean Income: 1947 to 1995."
Note: Changes in college costs as a percentage of family income from 1980 to 1995 are shown as percentage point changes. Calculations of tuition and cost of attendance as a percentage of median family income are the author's and are based on median income for families whose heads were 45 to 54 years old.

of reach for all except the most affluent, short of taking out loans and/or receiving other financial aid.[21]

INDEPENDENT STUDENTS AND AFFORDABILITY

Beginning in the mid-1980s and continuing into the 1990s, most undergraduate enrollment growth was among two groups: older, part-time students and women. College participation rates among recent high school graduates increased from 50 to 60 percent between 1980 and 1990, offsetting some of the enrollment losses that would otherwise have occurred as the 18-to-24-year-old cohort of traditional college students shrank in size. However, the continued aging of the baby-boom generation produced a tremendous increase in the size of the 25-to-34-year-old cohort and the 35-years-old-and-older cohort. Even though the college participation rates of these cohorts were much lower and did not increase appreciably, sheer growth in the size of the cohorts led to a substantial increase in the enrollment of older, part-time students. Between 1980 and 1995, the number of part-time undergraduates increased by 900,000, while the number of full-time undergraduates grew by 800,000. During the same period, the number of undergraduate men increased by over 400,000, or by 8 percent, while the number of women jumped by nearly 1.4 million, or almost 25 percent.[22]

Students over 24 years old were prominently represented in the ranks of part-time undergraduates, making up 63 percent of the total number of part-timers (see Table 2). They also made up over 90 percent of part-time graduate and professional students. For financial aid purposes, students over 24 years old are considered independent or self-supporting. Not surprisingly, for the 60 per 1,000 of that age group who did enroll as undergraduates, most enrolled part-time, continued working while attending, and reflected a wide range of economic circumstances. While some 14 percent had incomes of $50,000 or more, 29 percent had incomes below $10,000 and over half had incomes of less than $20,000. Two-thirds of those in the lowest income range received financial aid and so did over half of those in the $10,000 to $20,000 income range. Many independent undergraduates were struggling financially and heavily reliant on work and financial aid to help meet college costs.[23]

FINANCIAL AID AND EDUCATIONAL OPPORTUNITY

Over half of all undergraduates and nearly two-thirds of all full-time undergraduates currently receive some financial aid to help them meet the costs of higher education (see Tables 8 and 9). This aid is particularly important to full-time undergraduates, whether they are younger, dependent students or older and self-supporting. Over 86 percent of dependent undergraduates from families with incomes below $20,000 receive financial aid averaging almost $7,200. Nearly 71 percent of them receive Pell Grants and almost half borrow to help pay for their education. Among dependent students from families with incomes between $20,000 and $40,000, more than three-fourths receive some aid, 42 percent receive Pell Grants, and over half borrow. For the lowest-income independent students attending full-time, over 88 percent receive financial aid, three-fourths receive Pell Grants, and 57 percent borrow to help pay for college. The percentage of students receiving financial aid goes down as income increases, and Pell Grants are most heavily concentrated among the lowest-income students. Yet financial need is relative, not absolute. Because students from middle- and upper-income families are more likely to attend four-year institutions, especially private ones, than those from lower-income families, the average amount of aid received drops much more slowly as incomes increase than the percentage receiving Pell Grants.

TABLE 8.   *Income Distribution and Reliance on Financial Aid: All Undergraduates by Dependency Status, 1995-96*

Estimated Parental or Personal Income	Percentage of Undergraduates	Percentage Receiving Aid	Average Amount for Those Receiving Aid	Percentage Receiving Pell Grants	Percentage Receiving Loans
Dependent	**49.2%**	**50.9%**	**$5,923**	**18.5%**	**30.1%**
Less than $20,000	9.3	70.2	5,799	56.7	35.2
$20,000 to $39,999	11.2	60.3	6,111	30.9	37.4
$40,000 to $59,999	11.2	47.4	6,009	3.1	32.2
$60,000 to $79,999	8.2	42.5	5,809	0.1	26.6
$80,000 to $99,999	4.1	37.6	5,945	0.0	23.1
$100,000 and above	5.2	27.5	5,536	0.0	12.2
Independent	**50.8**	**48.5**	**3,915**	**24.7**	**20.5**
Less than $9,999	14.8	67.4	4,763	52.0	33.7
$10,000 to $19,999	11.5	50.6	3,916	24.2	23.1
$20,000 to $29,999	8.3	41.9	3,333	18.3	15.4
$30,000 to $49,999	9.0	36.3	3,020	6.0	12.1
$50,000 and above	7.2	29.3	2,235	0.0	5.8

Source: U.S. Department of Education, NCES, *NPSAS: 1995-96 Undergraduates,* Tables 2, 5, 8, August 1997.

TABLE 9.   *Income Distribution and Reliance on Financial Aid Among Full-Time Undergraduates by Dependency Status, 1995-96*

Estimated Parental or Personal Income	Percentage of Full-Time Undergraduates	Percentage Receiving Aid	Average Amount for Those Receiving Aid	Percentage Receiving Pell Grants	Percentage Receiving Loans
Dependent	**73.8%**	**64.8%**	**$6,938**	**22.6%**	**40.7%**
Less than $20,000	12.8	86.5	7,198	70.7	48.7
$20,000 to $39,999	16.5	78.0	7,258	42.0	50.9
$40,000 to $59,999	16.5	63.2	6,913	4.4	44.2
$60,000 to $79,999	12.7	56.3	6,455	0.0	36.6
$80,000 to $99,999	6.3	50.4	6,358	0.0	32.4
$100,000 and above	9.0	34.3	6,051	0.0	15.6
Independent	**26.2**	**78.6**	**6,587**	**51.1**	**50.2**
Less than $9,999	12.0	88.3	7,051	74.8	57.0
$10,000 to $19,999	6.0	78.5	6,310	42.8	50.7
$20,000 to $29,999	3.4	71.7	6,065	38.8	44.2
$30,000 to $49,999	3.0	62.6	6,420	17.9	41.4
$50,000 and above	1.9	55.0	4,597	0.0	29.2

Source: U.S. Department of Education NCES, *NPSAS: 1995-96 Undergraduates,* "Income Distribution of Undergraduates in 1995-96," Tables 9 and 10, August 1997.

UNDERGRADUATE ENROLLMENT IN THE FUTURE
AND THE ROLE OF PELL GRANTS

The implications of these family income and financial aid patterns for access to higher education in the future are profound. Unless a much greater proportion of low-income and minority youth gain access to and succeed in higher education, there will be little improvement in their general economic positions or incomes. Furthermore, significantly fewer African-American and Hispanic children come from families with sufficient financial resources for them to attend college unless they receive financial aid. The poorest 60 percent of African-American and Hispanic families have incomes that are at or below those of the poorest 40 percent of white families. More than three-quarters of current full-time undergraduates from families with such incomes receive financial aid. Even if college costs grow no more rapidly than family incomes over the next 15 years, changes in the country's ethnic composition over the same period mean that a much larger proportion of the college-age population will require financial aid if they are to have access to a college education. If college costs continue to increase at rates several percentage points above inflation and growth in family income, the overall percentage of students requiring financial aid will increase even more dramatically.

Just to educate the same proportion of the population as in 1995, nearly 13.5 million undergraduate students will need to enroll in 2005 and 14.3 million in 2010. That represents an increase of 1.2 million students in 2005 and over two million in 2010. Many factors will exert pressure on college participation rates: rising college costs; the sharp increase in competition for budget resources that public universities face from health care, social services, K-12 education, and prisons; competitive pressures in the global economy and stagnating earnings patterns for many individuals and families; and major shifts in the age and ethnic composition of the population. Given the profound shifts in the ethnic composition of the future college-aged population; the substantial proportion of African-American and Hispanic populations with considerably below-average or poverty-level incomes; and the current course-taking, academic preparation, and high school graduation patterns among these same groups, considerable forward strides will be needed at every step just to prevent the overall college participation and graduation rates from falling.

The two biggest challenges to expanding the college participation rates of low-income and minority students are: (1) improving the academic preparation of students to undertake college-level work, and (2) over-coming the barriers created by inadequate financial resources to pay for a college education. These two challenges are actually closely linked and both were recognized as explicit goals of the Pell Grant program when it was created 25 years ago. It was intended to provide both motivation and the promise of essential financial resources for low-income students.

Strategies for expanding educational opportunity will fall short if they concentrate on only one of these two dimensions of the problem. The most effective outreach and academic preparation efforts emphasize hard work, discipline, sacrifice, skill building, college-preparatory course sequences in middle school and high school, and high achievement. At the same time, the TRIO programs and the most effective institutional outreach efforts recognize that, without providing assurance to low-income and minority students that the financial resources they will need for their college education will be available, many of the personal sacri-fices required to prepare successfully for college can seem pointless. Without such assurances, the expense of a college education often appears beyond reach and students may all too easily become discouraged.

The National Advisory Committee on Student Financial Assistance, in a letter to Congress on reauthorization of the Higher Education Act, "found that progress toward the federal government's primary role in higher education—promoting equal access for low- and middle-income youth—has seriously stalled; and that a renewed commitment to at-risk students is required to position our nation for the 21st century."[24] To close the participation gap between rich and poor, the Advisory Committee called for clearly defined goals, increased funding for finan-cial aid, "quantum improvements in the quality of information provid-ed to students, parents and counselors about academic preparedness, college costs and financial aid," and better ways for federal aid dollars to leverage more state grant support.

Unfortunately, in the Taxpayer Relief Act of 1997, the federal gov-ernment chose to commit more resources in the form of tax benefits for middle- and upper-middle-income students ($12 to $15 billion annual-ly when fully phased in) than for the Pell Grant program, which assists low-income students ($5.4 billion in 1995-96 and $7.3 billion in 1997-98). Furthermore, it is ironic that the former effort is labeled the "Hope Scholarship" when those who are most in need of both hope and finan-cial assistance generally will not benefit from the tax breaks and will receive instead a modest increase in the Pell Grant. While the increase of $300 in the Pell Grant maximum in 1998-99 is the largest single-year increase since 1975-76, it only begins to restore the purchasing power of the Pell Grant that has been lost over the past 15 years.

If the nation hopes to educate 1.2 million more undergraduate students in 2005 and over two million more in 2010 (the numbers required to maintain the same percentage currently enrolled), 600,000 more Pell Grants will be needed in 2005 and 800,000 more in 2010. Furthermore, the maximum grant will need to be increased steadily. But even that may not be enough, because to reach these projected undergraduate enrollment levels, substantially larger percentages of young African-American, Hispanic, and other low-income students must enroll, and the vast majority of these future students will come from families with far fewer resources than today's students.

To provide real educational opportunity and ensure broad participation in postsecondary education will require a major financial commitment and a tremendous resolve to invest more in this nation's youth—a level of commitment to educational opportunity that this country has not yet exhibited. Lester Thurow has observed, "Today knowledge and skills now stand alone as the only source of comparative advantage" for both individuals and nations. He concludes:

> In the era ahead countries have to make the investments in knowledge and skills that will create a set of man-made brainpower industries that will allow their citizens to have high wages and a high standard of living. . . . Man-made brainpower industries are not a birthright. No country acquires these industries without effort and without making the investments necessary to create them.[25]

The Pell Grant is the proper vehicle for such an investment. A reinvigorated and expanded Pell Grant program with much larger grants and a more explicit commitment of aid to all low-income students who prepare themselves for success in college will help provide the motivation for future students to do so. The future is hardly on automatic pilot and success will require a carefully coordinated approach with major investments in financial aid and greatly improved academic preparation and support services if current participation levels are to be sustained, let alone improved. Anything less would be a major human tragedy and the future social and economic costs of that failure would be enormous.

SAMUEL M. KIPP III *is the head of Kipp Research and Consulting, a firm specializing in higher education finance, strategic planning, and policy analysis for colleges, states, and financial institutions. His career has included nine years as executive director of the California Student Aid Commission and eight years conducting policy research for the California Postsecondary Education Commission. He received his B.A. and M.A. degrees from the University of California, Davis, and his Ph.D. in history from Princeton University.*

NOTES

1. Lester Thurow, *The Future of Capitalism: How Today's Economic Forces Shape Tomorrow's World* (New York: William Morrow & Company, 1996), 8–9.

2. Paul Campbell, *Population Projections for States by Age, Sex, Race, and Hispanic Origin: 1995-2025* (Washington, D.C.: U.S. Census Bureau, October 1996), 54–55.

3. Western Interstate Commission for Higher Education (WICHE) and College Board, *Knocking at the College Door: Projections of High School Graduates by State and Race/Ethnicity, 1996–2012* (Boulder, CO: WICHE, 1998).

4. Campbell, *Population Projections*, 16.

5. Ibid, 60–67.

6. U.S. Department of Education, National Center for Education Statistics, *Projections of Education Statistics to 2005, Projections to 2006, Projections to 2007, and Projections to 2008* (Washington, D.C.: U.S. Government Printing Office, 1995, 1996, 1997, and 1998).

7. "Predicted Growth in Enrollment Hasn't Occurred in Some States," *Chronicle of Higher Education*, August 15, 1997.

8. *Education Week* and Pew Foundation, *Quality Counts 1996: The State of the States*, Executive Summary, 1996, 3.

9. U.S. Department of Education, National Center for Education Statistics, *Dropout Rates in the United States: 1995* (Washington, D.C.: U.S. Government Printing Office, 1997).

10. Ibid, vi–ix; Thurow, *Future of Capitalism*, 94–95.

11. USDE, NCES, *Dropout Rates*, 23; Campbell, *Population Projections*, 60–67.

12. U.S. Department of Education, National Center for Education Statistics, *National Longitudinal Study of 1988*, Third Follow-up Survey (Washington, D.C.: U.S. Government Printing Office, 1994), Tables 19–23; U.S. Department of Education, National Center for Education Statistics, *Digest of Education Statistics 1996* (Washington, D.C.: U.S. Government Printing Office, 1996), Table 179.

13. College Board, *College-Bound Seniors: 1997 Profiles of SAT and Achievement Test Takers*, National Report (New York: College Entrance Examination Board, 1997); College Board, *College-Bound Seniors: 1996 Profiles of SAT and Achievement Test Takers*, National Report (New York: College Entrance Examination Board, 1996); ACT Press Release, August 1997.

14. U.S. Department of Education, NCES, *National Education Longitudinal Study 1988,* Third Follow-Up Survey (Washington, D.C.: 1994).

15. USDE, NCES, *Digest,* Table 309.

16. U.S. Bureau of the Census, "Historical Income Tables—Persons" in *Current Population Survey* (Washington, D.C.: U.S. Government Printing Office, 1996), Tables P-4a and F-11; Thurow, 22–25.

17. U.S. Bureau of the Census, "Historical Income Tables – Families" in *Current Population Survey* (Washington, D.C.: U.S. Government Printing Office, 1996), Tables F-1, F-2, and F-11.

18. U.S. Bureau of the Census, "Household and Family Characteristics: March 1995" in *Current Population Survey* (Washington, D.C.: U.S. Government Printing Office, 1996), 1,2,7.

19. U.S. Bureau of the Census, *Income and Poverty: 1994 Poverty Summary* (Washington, D.C.: U.S. Government Printing Office, 1996), Table F.

20. USDE, NCES, Digest, Table 309; College Board, *Trends in Student Aid: 1985-1995* (New York: College Entrance Examination Board, 1995); U.S. Bureau of the Census, "Historical Income Tables—Families," Table F11.

21. Sandy Baum, "Comments," in *A Summary of the Sallie Mae Education Institute's Forum on College Affordability,* July 1997, 2–5.

22. USDE, NCES, *Digest,* Table 181; U.S. Department of Education, National Center for Education Statistics, *Enrollment: Fall 1995* (Washington, D.C.: U.S. Government Printing Office, 1997), Table I-4.

23. U.S. Department of Education, National Center for Education Statistics, *NPSAS: 1995-96 Undergraduate Students* (Washington, D.C.: U.S. Government Printing Office, August 1997), Table 5.

24. National Advisory Committee on Student Financial Assistance, Letter to Representative William Goodling, May 1, 1997.

25. Thurow, *Future of Capitalism,* 68–71.

Achieving the Initial Purposes of the Pell Grant Program

Arthur M. Hauptman

Abstract. *Senator Pell's original vision of providing at-risk youth with early and certain knowledge that they could afford to go to college has not been realized. The common explanations for why Pell Grants and other student aid have not been more successful in this mission center on the need for more money. But more financial aid alone is not the answer. To be successful, public efforts must also include support services, mentoring, and individualized attention to overcome the substantial obstacles that disadvantaged youth face in making the transition from school to college. Private early intervention efforts over the past decade have had considerable success, which the federal government should try to replicate. Toward this end, this paper recommends five changes in Pell Grants, TRIO, and other programs under Title IV of the Higher Education Act.*

One of the principal purposes of the Pell Grant program when it was first established in 1972 was to raise the aspirations of disadvantaged students by assuring them as early as the sixth grade that a defined amount of financial aid would be available to them when they were ready to go to college. While the Pell Grant program over the past quarter century has helped millions of students enroll in postsecondary education and has become an essential piece of the federal financial aid system, Senator Claiborne Pell's initial vision of providing at-risk youth with early and certain knowledge that they could afford to go to college has not been realized.

Most of the explanations for why Pell Grants and other student aid programs have not been more successful in helping low-income and minority students bridge the gap in college participation typically center on the need for more money. For one, the Pell Grant never became an entitlement, leaving the program vulnerable to annual appropriations wars. Second, the maximum Pell Grant award has not kept up with inflation, or with increases in college costs, thereby reducing the ability of the program to improve college participation rates. And third, proprietary school students have siphoned off funds that could have been used for students in more traditional academic programs.

While more funding would no doubt yield higher awards for targeted groups of students, there is increasing evidence that providing more money for Pell Grants is not the sole answer to raising the aspirations and college participation rates of at-risk youth. The past quarter century of experience makes it clear that Pell Grants alone are not sufficient to solve the problem. To be successful, it is apparent that public efforts must also include a wide range of support services and individualized attention to overcome the substantial obstacles that disadvantaged youth face in making the transition from school to college.

This paper examines why the original purpose of the Pell Grants has not been achieved and what steps could be taken now to realize that original vision. The first section looks at a number of traditional explanations, most centering on the need for more money, for why Pell Grants and the other federal student aid programs have not been more effective in raising the college participation rates of traditionally underserved groups of students. The second section examines the success over the past decade of private early-intervention strategies in an attempt to identify how Pell Grants and other student aid and support services programs could be modified to be more effective, while requiring little if any new federal funding.

THE TRADITIONAL EXPLANATIONS

In its 25 years of existence, the Pell Grant has become a key federal student assistance program. Other contributors to this book state that Pell Grants have become the critical difference in whether many nontraditional groups of students are able to further their educational goals. For the growing number of older students seeking training or retraining, Pell Grants are now a primary form of assistance. Pell Grants have also become an essential part of many Department of Labor training programs by providing stipends that allow recipients to support themselves while they are engaged in training activities. Pell Grants also were the primary source of financing for the postsecondary education and training of prisoners before they were made ineligible.

The evidence is less clear, however, when we examine the effect that the Pell Grant, and student aid more generally, has had on the participation of at-risk students in postsecondary education and training. Pell Grants certainly are an essential part of financing short-term training in proprietary schools and community colleges. A high proportion of students participating in vocational training receive Pell Grants, and nearly half of all Pell Grant dollars are awarded to students enrolled either in proprietary schools or community colleges. These statistics suggest that Pell Grants have played and continue to play a significant role in the financing of postsecondary vocational training.

Less progress has been made with respect to the participation of traditional college-age students in academic programs. To be sure, the college participation rates of new high school graduates from low-income families have substantially increased over time. For example, the proportion of high school graduates from low-income families enrolling in college in the fall following their graduation rose by 50 percent over a 20-year period, from 30 percent in 1975 to 45 percent in 1995. Despite this improvement, however, the gap in college participation rates between students from low-income families and those from higher-income families widened over that same 20-year period, while the college participation rates of students from middle- and upper-income families increased more rapidly than those of students from lower-income families.[1]

Many factors other than the availability of Pell Grants have influenced these changing patterns of college-going behavior. The elimination of the military draft in the 1970s was certainly an important factor for males of traditional college age. So was the availability of the GI Bill for those students who served in the armed forces. The patterns of state support for higher education and the effect they have on the tuition that public institutions charge are probably far more important in determining who goes to college than Pell Grants. For that matter, given the growing reliance on loans to finance college attendance, Pell Grants are probably not even the most important form of federal aid in explaining college participation rates. Nonetheless, there is a tendency either to give Pell Grants the credit for the improvement in college participation rates or the blame for the widening gap between students from low- and high-income families.

Many reasons have traditionally been put forward to explain why Pell Grants and the other federal student aid programs have not been more successful in encouraging disadvantaged students to go to college.

The Pell Grant never became the federal entitlement it was supposed to be. An essential element of the initial vision of the Pell Grant was that eventually it would become an entitlement like Social Security. The notion was that this would provide the assurance to students that aid would be available when they were ready to go to college. Much of the higher education community's lobbying efforts concerning reauthorization of the Higher Education Act over the past quarter-century have focused on the goal of making the Pell Grant an entitlement.

Although achieving entitlement status certainly would enhance the Pell Grant's position among federal aid programs, the fact is that the Pell Grant has been treated as though it is an entitlement. Moreover, making the Pell Grant an entitlement would not assure students while in an early grade that aid would be available to them when they were ready for college. That is, making the Pell Grant an entitlement program does not translate into a guarantee of aid for an individual student. Without such an individualized, early guarantee of assistance, it is difficult to imagine Pell Grants producing a radical change in the college-going behavior of at-risk students.

Inadequate program funding has led to declines in the real value of the maximum Pell Grant award. Another frequent assertion is that inadequate funding is the only barrier keeping the Pell Grant program from accomplishing all that it was intended to do. This argument is linked to the fact that the maximum Pell Grant award has not kept pace with either the general rate of inflation or the much more rapid increase in college costs. Even the increase in the maximum award to $3,000 for the academic year 1997-98 still falls far short of the real value of the maximum Pell award when it peaked twenty years ago.[2]

The thrust of this argument is that if sufficient funding were provided, the real value of the Pell maximum award could be restored and the program could then meet initial expectations. But this argument flies in the face of the actual funding history—total federal appropriations for Pell Grants have grown in real terms over time when adjusted for inflation. The pattern has been one in which Pell Grant funding is substantially increased for one or two years, often around the time of a presidential election, then the appropriations fall in real terms for several years, and then the cycle begins again with another real increase in funding. With the big hikes in funding over the past two years, appropriations for Pell Grants now exceed $7 billion, the highest level ever in real terms.

If funding is at its highest level ever, why then is the maximum award so much lower than it was in the 1970s? This seeming paradox has occurred because eligibility for Pell Grants periodically has been stretched up the income scale to maintain political support for the program. These expansions have been accomplished in a variety of ways. The rate at which family income is assessed to determine ability to pay has been reduced in several instances, thereby increasing income eligibility. In 1992, a family's home equity was removed as a consideration in the calculation of ability to pay, making more families with higher incomes eligible for Pell Grants.

The net result of the efforts over the years to expand eligibility is that the maximum award grew far more slowly than the overall funding of the program, leading program advocates to complain that the maximum award was not keeping pace with inflation. This is an old shell game in many domestic programs: broaden eligibility for a program and then complain when funds do not grow as fast as the number of eligible recipients. While spreading the benefits more widely makes for good politics, it also detracts from the effort to target aid to those who need it most.

In the case of the Pell Grant and other student aid programs, there is an added twist to the traditional shell game. With respect to federal student aid, the argument is also made that funding has not kept pace with increases in college costs. While this is most certainly true—college tuition has grown at twice the rate of inflation—it also raises the question of whether it is the federal government's role to keep up with what may be excessive increases in tuition and other charges. It also opens the higher education community to criticisms regarding whether student aid programs are fueling tuition growth.

Proprietary school students are siphoning funds from students in academic programs. One of the more remarkable developments in the Pell Grant program over its first quarter century, and in federal student aid programs more generally, has been the growth in the proportion of dollars going to recipients in the proprietary sector of postsecondary education. When proprietary school students were first made eligible for federal student aid programs in 1972, even the staunchest advocates of this change probably would have had difficulty imagining how much aid would eventually go to students in this sector. At its peak in the late 1980s, as much as one-quarter of all Pell Grant dollars went to proprietary school students, and the proportion was similar if not larger in federal student loan programs.[3]

This growth has led many to suggest over the years that a new set of programs should be established for proprietary school students separate from those for students in academic programs. This issue, like the questions of making Pell Grants an entitlement and ensuring that the maximum award keeps up with inflation, is ultimately an issue of money. Every dollar that proprietary school students receive is a dollar out of the pocket of students in more traditional nonprofit institutions.

Like making Pell Grants an entitlement, however, separating out proprietary school students from traditional student aid programs probably will not contribute substantially to helping the Pell Grant reach its initial objective of raising the aspirations of at-risk students. It is difficult to imagine that reducing student eligibility for the program would not also result in reduced funding. Moreover, proprietary schools serve a disproportionate number of at-risk students. Removing these institutions from the Pell Grant program reduces the range of options open to those students.

Another possible explanation: Expectations are too high. There are a number of plausible explanations other than lack of resources for why the Pell Grant program has not been more successful. These other explanations are more closely related to the expectations that are now placed on the Pell Grant program and have less to do with how much funding it and other federal student aid programs have received over time.

In its 25-year existence, the Pell Grant has grown into a program that provides $7 billion annually to more than 4 million students. As such, it has become the principal source of federal grant assistance, providing more than 5 percent of the total cost of attendance for all postsecondary students in the country. Although this growth over time in Pell Grant funding is dwarfed by the increased reliance on student loans as a source of funding for college—loans now pay for one-third of all costs of attendance—nonetheless Pell Grants have solidified their position as a foundation of the federal aid structure.

As a foundation program, the Pell Grant has many constituencies and many goals. It is the base on which all other aid programs are built. It is supposed to open opportunity for millions of disadvantaged youth, but it also has become critical in providing older, nontraditional students with the opportunity to go to college. And over time, as has already been discussed, Pell Grant eligibility has been expanded up the income scale to help ensure the political viability of the program.

This diversity in the constituencies and goals of the Pell Grant, while laudable in many respects, has had the undeniable result of watering down the effectiveness of the program for the students who were supposed to be its primary beneficiaries—traditional college-age students from impoverished circumstances who could not continue their education without substantial amounts of financial assistance.

The conclusion from all this may be that a program that seeks to accomplish as much as Pell Grants cannot and should not be expected to achieve the initial goal of raising the aspirations of disadvantaged youth. Instead, what may be needed is a separate effort that is more explicitly focused on the needs and the situation of at-risk students.

REPLICATING PRIVATE EARLY-INTERVENTION EFFORTS

Over the past decade, hundreds if not thousands of private early-intervention efforts have been initiated as philanthropists, corporations, and others have sought to address the question of how to improve college participation and completion rates among the most needy in our society. From what started as a few individuals offering hope to classes of grade-school students in impoverished areas, private early-intervention efforts have expanded to include a much broader range of activities intended to prepare disadvantaged students to do college-level work and provide them with enough funds to assure sufficient financial aid for college if they make the grade in high school.

Those private early-intervention efforts that have been in place long enough to have had their results evaluated appear to be having a high degree of success in increasing the proportion of students who complete high school, are ready to go to college when they receive their high school diploma, and graduate from college. Assessments of these efforts suggest that their success is a function of two critical components:[4]

- First, they guarantee at-risk youth as early as grade school that adequate financial aid for college will be available. Many private early-intervention activities assure students as they leave grade school or in middle school that the full costs of college will be covered if they succeed in completing high school and gaining admission to college. This has the effect of raising students' aspirations because they know the money will be there if they are ready to do the work. The positive effects of this guarantee of assistance cannot be overestimated.

- Second, private early-intervention efforts typically provide a great deal of individualized attention to students in the form of mentoring, tutoring, and other support services. In many instances, individuals from the community volunteer to serve as mentors and tutors. All the existing assessments of private early-intervention programs indicate that this kind of individualized attention is critical to ensure that students are ready for college when they finish high school, thereby allowing them to benefit from the financial aid guarantee.

Thus far, however, neither the federal government nor state governments have been able to replicate and institutionalize the success of private early-intervention efforts. A primary obstacle in this regard is that government programs tend to be broad-based, making it difficult to tailor them to the specific needs of particular students.

For government programs to be more successful in influencing the college-going behavior of at-risk students, it will be necessary for them to emulate the critical features of private early-intervention efforts, including: targeting assistance to the most at-risk students, guaranteeing the availability of aid as early as possible, and providing support services that complement the aid that students receive.

It is a premise of this paper that exploring options in which private early intervention is emulated at the federal and state levels will in the long run prove more fruitful than pursuing the notion of a Pell Grant entitlement or substantial expansion in the funding of Pell Grants.

This paper suggests five changes in Pell Grants and in the array of federal student aid and support services efforts to enable the federal government to replicate the success of private early-intervention strategies. Two of these suggestions relate directly to the policies and operation of the Pell Grant program; the other three are directed at aspects of federal efforts other than Pell Grants.

First, eligibility for Pell Grants should be more explicitly focused on students from the lowest-income families and should not be expanded further up the income scale. The federal government should rely instead on new tax provisions and on loans as the principal federal policies for keeping college affordable for middle-income students and their families.

As already discussed, the history of the Pell Grant program shows that there has been continual pressure to expand eligibility up the income scale to maintain the political viability of the program. While this strategy has had the desired effect of maintaining necessary political support, it also has had the undesirable effect of diluting the impact of Pell Grants on students from the lowest-income families.

The newly enacted education tax provisions provide an opportunity to move away from the traditional trade-off between providing higher awards for students from low-income families and expanding Pell Grant eligibility for middle-income students. Whatever one thinks of these new provisions, they will provide unprecedented amounts of aid to help middle-class families offset tuition-related expenses.

Families with incomes between $40,000 and $80,000 will receive the bulk of the benefits from the two new tuition tax credits. Students from families with incomes less than $40,000 will benefit less from them, either because they do not pay enough income tax to take advantage of the credit or because the Pell Grants they receive will be subtracted from tuition to determine eligibility for the credits. Efforts during the debate over the credits to distribute them more progressively, such as making them refundable or by not taking a student's Pell Grant into account in calculating them, were rebuffed. Higher-income families will not benefit as much from the new tax credits because eligibility begins to phase out at family incomes of $80,000 and families earning more than $100,000 will not be eligible at all.

Given who is likely to benefit from the tax credits, it makes even more sense to refocus the Pell Grants on those students who most need the help—those whose family resources are insufficient to meet the growing costs of college yet who will not be eligible for the tax credits because they or their families do not pay enough income tax to qualify.

Federal policies seem to be moving in the opposite direction, however. Over the past two years, the maximum Pell Grant award has been increased from $2,470 to $3,000. These increases have appropriately been lauded as a sign that the federal government is now willing to increase its commitment to help the neediest students because raising the maximum award will indeed provide more aid to the lowest-income students.

Under current award rules, however, raising the maximum by more than $500 over the past two years also increased the number of Pell Grant recipients by 300,000 to 400,000, an increase of roughly 10 percent. The bulk of these new recipients come from families with incomes between $40,000 and $50,000. It would have been better policy, in my opinion, not to have brought these new students into the Pell Grant program, because they are the same students who will be the principal beneficiaries of the new tuition tax credits.

Second, the Pell Grant application process and form should be simplified and students should be provided with earlier information about their eligibility. This could be accomplished by revising the Pell Grant award rules and prorating the maximum award for part-time students.

The concept behind Pell Grants when they were first debated in the early 1970s was to design a national program in which students would be able to fill out a simple application form as early as the sixth grade to find out how much aid they would be eligible to receive when they were ready for college. In the intervening quarter century, however, none of these concepts—a simple application form, early knowledge, and a certain award—have been realized.

The idea of informing students of how much aid they would receive regardless of where they went to college fell by the wayside when a provision was added at the end of the 1972 debate limiting awards to one-half the cost of attendance. This provision was added to prevent community college students from receiving their entire cost of attendance in the form of grant assistance. But another effect of the cost limitation was that students had to know where they were going to enroll before they could be sure how much aid they would receive.

Although the 1992 reauthorization removed the cost limitation (by then at 60 percent of costs) and set the amount of nontuition cost at a standard level equal to the maximum award, cost of attendance is still a factor in the Pell award calculation for part-time students.[5] As a result, cost of attendance remains part of the Pell Grant calculation for all students even though this provision affects the size of the award for only about 1 percent of all recipients.

The concept of providing students with information about their Pell Grant eligibility as early as the sixth grade was thwarted when it was decided that eligibility for Pell Grants and other federal aid would be based on financial information for the most recent year available. This view also prevailed in the most recent reauthorization when the Clinton administration's proposal to use income information for the year prior to that in which students apply for aid was rejected.

The idea of a simple application form for federal aid was the victim of the simplicity-versus-equity dilemma that emerges in debates over the tax code and many other domestic programs. In these debates, those arguing for a simple form that everybody can understand often lose out to those who argue that more items on the form provide additional information that allows for greater refinement in the treatment of people in different circumstances. Asking families about various kinds of assets, nontaxable income, and other things may provide for greater fairness in the system, but at the cost of greater complexity and confusion.

There are good reasons to require information on cost of attendance to determine the size of the award, to use data on income for the most recent year available, and to expand the number of items required on the federal financial aid form. But there are negative consequences as well—confusion and uncertainty among students and their families regarding the financial aid process, which may lead to fewer applications for financial aid. The most recent reauthorization did not help in this regard. Advocates for more simplicity were systematically defeated by those arguing for more equity (and as a consequence, greater complexity).

Senator Pell's conception of a simple form, early information on aid eligibility, and aid awards that do not vary with cost deserves urgent reconsideration. The greater equity realized by collecting more information, in my opinion, is not worth the cost of greater complexity and less certainty among students about their eligibility for aid. In addition, replacing the need restriction in the current award formula with a provision that prorates the maximum award for less-than-full-time students would mean cost of attendance would no longer be a factor in determining the size of a student's award. As a result, the government could publicize that students would receive the same amount of aid no matter what college they attended.

Third, the federal government should establish and fund college savings accounts for at-risk students whose families cannot afford to save for college. To be most effective, these new savings accounts, which could be supplemented by government or private contributions, should not count against students' eligibility for financial aid.

One of the primary goals of the recent tax legislation was to encourage families to save more for college. But the new savings provisions by and large will not help families whose income is so low that they do not pay much in taxes. For these families, saving for college is not a realistic expectation because most of them simply do not have the funds to save as do their middle-class counterparts.

To provide greater assurance of funds for individual at-risk students, the government should consider establishing college savings accounts in the name of the student, to be used only for meeting tuition and related expenses when the student is ready to go to college. For low-income students whose families do not have the resources to save for college, the federal government could initially fund these interest-bearing accounts by depositing $500—the same amount as the new child tax credit and the same amount that middle-income parents may deposit in educational IRAs—for sixth-grade students whose family's tax liability is less than the credit. This initial allocation could then be supplemented through contributions from government or philanthropy. To ensure the maximum effectiveness of these accounts for this group of students, the funds thus reserved for them should not detract from their eligibility for Pell Grants or other forms of federal student financial aid.

Fourth, a small proportion of Pell Grant appropriations should be set aside to encourage institutions to provide support services and other assistance designed to improve the preparation and success rates of students from lower-income families. To achieve this end, these funds should be distributed on the basis of the number of Pell Grant recipients an institution graduates.

It is increasingly apparent that putting more dollars in the hands of students is a necessary but not sufficient answer for increasing the college participation and retention rates of at-risk students. An alarming problem in U.S. higher education is the growing number of students who arrive at college without adequate preparation and who therefore require remediation. For those students, improving the K-12 education system is essential, but it also critical to pay more attention to the support services that prepare them to get into and through college.

The TRIO programs represent the federal government's main effort to improve support services. But funding of the TRIO programs, which were created in the 1965 Higher Education Act and thus predate Pell Grants, has grown far more slowly than Pell Grants and other student aid programs. The TRIO programs now receive only about $500 million in annual funding, less than 5 percent of the total spent on federal grants, work-study, student loan subsidies, and student loan defaults. Moreover, TRIO has never evolved beyond categorical programs that fund institutions on competitive basis. As a result, they serve only a small proportion of students—10 percent or less—who are eligible to benefit from the services they provide.

One way to help ensure that support services are better funded would be to tie TRIO funding to Pell Grant funding. As funding for Pell Grants grows over time, so would funding for the support services provided through the TRIO programs. But many of those who are most closely associated with TRIO apparently believe that it will do better if it remains a separate line item in the appropriations legislation.

As an alternative, a small portion of Pell Grant appropriations (say 5 percent) could be provided directly to institutions in recognition of the importance of providing support services to improve access and retention. For this concept to work most effectively, however, institutions should not be required to use these funds for the purpose of providing support services. Instead, payments could be made to institutions on the basis of the number of Pell Grant recipients they graduate. Under this arrangement, institutions could use the funds in whatever way they thought best, but future payments would be determined by how well the institutions succeeded in enrolling and graduating Pell Grant recipients.

The growing number of remedial courses offered on college campuses is another indicator of the problem of underprepared students. New arrangements for funding remediation are needed so that students taking remedial courses no longer have to borrow as they now must to learn basic skills. This could be accomplished by shifting to a system in which students would no longer be charged tuition and could no longer borrow for the remedial courses they take. Instead, the providers of remediation would be paid on the basis of how well they perform in improving students' basic skills. Students taking remedial courses should still be eligible for Pell Grants, however, to help pay their living costs.

Fifth, the federal State Student Incentive Grant (SSIG) program should be merged with existing federal early-intervention efforts to create a federal matching program for states that establish qualified early-intervention programs. This new program should be structured to ensure that qualifying state efforts target at-risk students.

Federal policymakers tended to take the view that when it comes to student financial aid, the federal government can do it alone. Establishing Pell Grants as a foundation program with no recognition in the award formula of other available forms of federal, state, and institutional aid is one example of this philosophy. Another example is that the predominant student loan programs are federally guaranteed and subsidized despite the fact that they were modeled after preexisting state programs. The difficulty in narrowing the gap in the college participation rates of lower-income and minority students, however, demonstrates that states must be more of a partner in the process if the college participation rates of at-risk students are to improve.

The SSIG program is an exception, an example of a federal program specifically designed to promote certain kinds of state behavior. Created in 1972 at the same time as the Pell Grant program, its purpose was to encourage states to establish need-based grant programs. The SSIG program is also an example of a federal effort that succeeded—every state now has such a program. It has since become a special revenue-sharing program, providing funds to states for activities that they already engage in.[6]

In 1992, the federal government enacted another program that seeks to encourage certain kinds of behavior on the part of the states. Based on initial reports of the success of private early-intervention efforts, the National Early Intervention Scholarship Program (NEISP) was designed to encourage states to establish early-intervention programs of their own. This initiative has never been adequately funded, however, and remains essentially a demonstration effort.

One approach to consider is a marriage of the NEISP and SSIG programs, thus creating a partnership that recognizes the importance of the states in the financial aid equation. Because the SSIG program has long since achieved its initial purpose, it could be redirected to encourage states to fund early-intervention efforts. To maximize the leverage of federal dollars in providing access for disadvantaged students, however, it would be best to require states to target at-risk populations to qualify for these funds.

CONCLUDING NOTE

While the Pell Grant program has accomplished much in its 25-year history, the goal of raising the aspirations and the college participation rates of at-risk youth remains elusive. The five suggestions outlined above could go a long way toward finally achieving this initial purpose of the Pell Grant program while not detracting from the many other good things that it does. As the program enters its second quarter century, this seems a worthwhile goal to renew.

ARTHUR M. HAUPTMAN *has been an independent public policy consultant specializing in higher education finance issues since 1981. He has written extensively on student aid, college costs, and trends in higher education expenditures and revenues. He previously served on the staff of the House Budget Committee and the Senate Committee on Labor and Human Resources. He received a B.A. in Economics from Swarthmore College and an M.B.A. from Stanford University.*

NOTES

1. Enrollment rates are from the U.S. Department of Commerce, Bureau of the Census, October Current Population Surveys.
2. See Table 1 in the Introduction to this book.
3. Statistics on the distribution of student aid by sector and the growth in student aid funding over time are from The College Board, *Trends in Student Aid: 1987 to 1997* (New York: College Entrance Examination Board, 1997).
4. Assessments of private early-intervention efforts thus far have been more anecdotal than systematic. Two volumes that have described and reviewed the effects of private early-intervention are Robert Fenske et al., *Early Intervention Programs: Opening the Door to Higher Education* (Washington, D.C.: George Washington University Press, 1997), and Arthur Levine and Jana Nidiffer, *Beating the Odds: How the Poor Get to College* (San Francisco: Jossey-Bass, 1996).
5. For purposes of the Pell Grant award formula, the 1992 reauthorization set nontuition expenses equal to the maximum award. Thus, if the maximum award is $3,000, full-time students have $3,000 added to their tuition to determine their total costs of attendance. For the high majority of students, their award is equal to the maximum grant minus their family contribution because need always exceeds this calculation. Only part-time students are potentially affected by the need part of the formula, that is, Pell Grant award equals the maximum minus family contribution not to exceed need (costs minus family contribution).
6. Because the SSIG appropriation falls far short of the matching funds called for in the formula, most states receive far less than what the match would be if the program were fully funded. As a result, funds are allocated to states mostly on the basis of their share of enrollments. Thus the SSIG program can be viewed as a special form of revenue sharing.

Priorities for Federal Student Aid Policy: Looking Beyond Pell Grants

Michael S. McPherson
and Morton Owen Schapiro

Abstract. *Real increases in net tuition have impaired higher education access and choice, principally for students from low-income families during the 1980s and 1990s. Yet student aid policy seems to be drifting away from need-based principles and becoming less responsive to those students with the least resources. Institutions, states, and the federal government should work together to restore the principles of need-based assistance that helped inspire the original Pell Grant program. Recovering a sense of teamwork in this effort will not happen overnight. But in the spirit of "imagination," policymakers should consider establishing a new federal grant program that would supplement the Pell Grant. For its students to be eligible for this program, a college or university would have to show that it was meeting a certain percentage of the financial need of its lower-income students. Thus the proposal rests on the notion that the federal government must recognize the incentives its policies create for individual colleges as well as states. Many variations on the specific design of such a program are possible. The important point is to try to get all the partners in the system to focus again on helping the neediest students to go to college.*

The Student Aid Game[1] includes an extensive analysis of evidence on trends in enrollment and financing in American higher education. From that analysis we draw three points that are important in setting the context for current policy discussions on higher education in the United States.

First, state governments have been providing a decreasing share of U.S. higher education revenues since the mid-1980s. There has been a dramatic reduction in the share of revenues provided by state governments through appropriations to public colleges and universities. States provided 43 percent of revenues in 1979-80 (ignoring financial aid provided by states) but only 33 percent of revenues in 1992-93. The share has likely fallen further since then. This sharp decline in state government contributions has been offset by an increase in the share of revenues provided by students and families through tuition—a share that rose from 26 percent in 1979-80 to 35 percent in 1992-93.

Declining state contributions have resulted in large part from sustained pressures on state budgets, the product of resistance to levying taxes on one hand and of increasing demands on states to finance elementary and secondary education, medical care, prisons, and other high-priority items on the other. Large percentage increases in tuition at public institutions, aimed at compensating for contractions in real state government support, have put pressure on families of moderate means and have certainly added to the political agitation for lower college costs and for more government support to defray those costs.

The second point is that while tuition has increased and support from state governments has diminished, federal student aid has not kept up with increasing costs. From 1986-87 to 1992-93, federal grants remained approximately constant in real value for low-income students attending private institutions. In light of the considerable real increase in gross tuition, this means that the percentage of tuition covered by federal financial aid for low-income students attending private institutions decreased considerably over time—from 22 percent in 1986-87 to only 16 percent in 1992-93. The number and amount of federal grants for low-income students attending public colleges and universities have increased slightly in real terms, but not enough to maintain the percentage contribution level of these grants to tuition. As a result, the percentage of tuition covered by federal financial aid for low-income students attending public institutions decreased from 68 percent in 1986-87 to 42 percent in 1992-93.

At the same time, the amount of federal loan money available to cover college costs has grown rapidly. Federal lending increased $9 billion in real dollars in the two years between 1992-93 and 1994-95. The two most important explanations for this growth were the introduction of unsubsidized loans and a set of changes in need analysis methodology introduced in the 1992 reauthorization of the Higher Education Act. Students receive interest subsidies on their loans only to the extent that they can be shown to have financial need. When Congress decided to write the need analysis rules directly into the 1992 legislation, it made those rules significantly more lenient with respect to middle- and upper-middle-income students. Most strikingly, a family's home equity was no longer counted as an asset. These changes mean that many families with children at public institutions who would not have qualified as needy under the old rules are now eligible for subsidized loans.

This recent pattern of declining real funding for federal grants coupled with rapid expansion in subsidized loans seems not to reflect a deliberate policy shift but rather the working out of budgetary constraints. Because grant funds are a form of discretionary spending, decline in their real value reflects the impact of the general squeeze on the federal budget. Guaranteed loans, by contrast, are an entitlement and so are not affected in the same way in the short run by budget battles. A partial reversal of the trend toward greater reliance on loans occurred in 1996, when Congress, in an election year, voted to increase the maximum Pell Grant from $2,470 to $2,700. The recent further increase to $3,000 was another positive step, although it would take a considerable additional effort by the federal government to restore the real value of the Pell Grant to the level reached almost two decades ago. In fact, between 1980 and 1994, tuition increased by 86 percent in real terms at the average public four-year college, by 77 percent at the average private four-year college, and by 70 percent at the average public two-year college. Despite the rise in the maximum Pell Grant award, its real value fell by 27 percent over that same period.

The third point is that, although more students are attending college than ever before, there are clear signs that the higher net costs of college are restricting the options of lower-income students. Participation in enrollment growth has been uneven. When we look at enrollment rates for white, African-American, and Hispanic high school graduates over time, we see that enrollment has grown more slowly for African Americans and Hispanics than for whites. The most likely reason for this is that African Americans and Hispanics have lower incomes on average than whites, and thus have been more vulnerable to rising net college costs. Other evidence[2] indicates that enrollment rates have grown much more slowly—or may even have fallen—for families in the bottom quartile of the income distribution than for families in the top three quartiles. In fact, the enrollment rate for financially dependent 18- and 19-year-old students from families in the top quarter of the income distribution increased from 68.7 percent in 1977-79 to 75.4 percent in 1991-93. At the same time, the enrollment rate for students from families in the middle half of the income distribution increased from 45 percent to 49.9 percent. During that same period, however, the enrollment rate for students from families in the bottom quarter of the income distribution actually fell from 26.3 percent to 25.5 percent.

There is also evidence that students from lower-income families who do attend college are finding their choices increasingly constrained by financial pressures. Smaller shares of students from middle- and upper-income families have chosen to attend community colleges since 1980, while the share of students from lower-income families attending these institutions has risen during this period. The share of students from the highest income group who began at community colleges declined from 14.5 percent to 8.6 percent while the share of students from the upper-middle-income group fell from 27.6 percent to 22.1 percent. In contrast, the share of students from the least affluent group who started at community colleges rose from 45.9 percent to 47.3 percent. It appears that in a number of states, the only financially viable option for many students from lower-income families is to live at home and attend the local community college. It is by no means a criticism of the education offered at community colleges to note that these lower-income students are being denied options that are available to their more affluent peers.

The background for current policy debates on U.S. higher education has been set by increases in tuition at public institutions driven by constrained state government budgets, the failure of federal student aid programs to keep pace with inflation in college costs, and an increase in federal loans relative to grants, with recent expansions in loans probably benefiting students with relatively high ability to pay.

Although it seems clear that the financial pressures that have resulted from these changes have had their strongest impact on lower-income students, they have certainly been felt by a politically vocal and influential group of middle- and upper-income families. Policy proposals introduced by the Clinton administration in 1996-97 were focused principally on responding to the cries arising from these same families, and the ultimate budget resolution reflected that political reality.

RECENT FEDERAL POLICY INITIATIVES

The most prominent policy proposals advanced by the Clinton administration and ultimately adopted as part of the budget for fiscal year 1998 were tuition tax credits. It makes sense to review the particulars of these provisions because there is every reason to believe that the incentive effects of such proposals are mightily affected by the details.

The centerpiece of the new education provisions, expected to cost about $40 billion over five years, is the Hope Scholarship/Lifetime Learning Credit, which took effect January 1, 1998. The Hope Scholarship credit applies to the first two years of higher education. It is equal to 100 percent of the first $1,000 in college tuition and fees and 50 percent of the next $1,000. Thus, the maximum value of the credit would be a cut in tax liability of $1,500 per year. Beginning with the student's junior year, Lifetime Learning Credits come into play, with a maximum value of $1,000 (20 percent of the first $5,000 in tuition, an amount that is scheduled to increase to $10,000 in 2002). In the cases of both credits, only those parents who pay income tax can benefit and the credits phase out for individuals with adjusted gross incomes between $40,000 and $50,000 and for couples with adjusted gross incomes between $80,000 and $100,000. Other parts of the budget dealing with higher education include an "Education IRA" that allows parents to contribute up to $500 per year (contributions are taxable but investment earnings are tax-deferred); the ability to withdraw money without penalty from regular IRAs to meet college expenses; deductibility of up to $1,000 in student loan interest; and an increase in the maximum value of the Pell Grant from $2,700 to $3,000 per year (if the Pell Grant fully covers tuition, the family is not eligible for the tuition tax credits described above).

Most of these policy provisions relate closely to the proposals offered by President Clinton and debated by higher education researchers and leaders. Aspects of the president's plan that were abandoned included the option for taxpayers to choose between the tax credit and a tax deduction of up to $10,000 per year and a requirement that to receive the tax credit in the second year of college, students would have to earn at least a B average in their first year.

Will these new tax provisions give colleges an incentive to raise tuition prices? In principle, some students could receive both a Pell Grant and a tax credit, worth a total of $4,500, which exceeds the cost of tuition at a large number of public institutions. In practice, few families could have incomes low enough to qualify for a maximum Pell Grant yet high enough to benefit from the tax credit. More realistically, there will certainly be families who will qualify for a combination of a Pell Grant and a tax credit that is worth less than $4,500 but is still more than tuition at many community colleges and some public four-year institutions. Under these rules, a nontrivial incentive for public institutions to capture federal dollars by raising tuition will be created. Whether such an incentive will outweigh political pressures to keep tuition down is unclear; probably the answer will be different in different states.

What about the likely impact of the tax credits on institutional and state financial aid? We suspect that here the incentive effects are likely to be quite strong.[3] The standard methodology for determining family ability to pay for college should take the added resources provided by these tax breaks into account in determining financial need. There are actually two different ways in which colleges and state student aid agencies might treat these added resources. One would be to view the increase in after-tax income simply as that: added after-tax earning power, similar to any other tax cut a family might receive. In that case the reduction in calculated family need would be a fraction of the increase in after-tax income, that fraction being determined by the marginal taxing rate within the student aid system. A family earning $60,000 to $80,000 per year that was eligible for state or institutional aid would be expected to contribute about 44 percent of the tax break in the form of increased family ability to pay. A second approach would be to treat the tax break as an added resource available to the student, much like an outside scholarship. In this case, standard methodology would say that all the added after-tax income should be devoted to educational expenses and the aid received from the state or the institution would be reduced dollar for dollar against the proceeds of the tax credit or deduction. No doubt colleges will vary in the fraction of tax-break dollars that they actually capture, but both typical practices and the logic of the need-based student aid system imply that a significant portion of these dollars will be absorbed by the institutions.

Our conclusion that colleges will substitute tax-break dollars for their own student aid dollars is different from the empirical findings in some of our earlier work, in which we reported that institutions increased their own aid spending when Pell Grant spending increased.[4] In that case, however, we suggested that this result was explained by the fact that colleges were induced by increased Pell Grant availability to recruit more needy students, who then received institutionally based aid as well as Pell Grants. Unfortunately, the tax breaks in the new bill are not targeted at the high-need students whose college-going behavior is most likely to be influenced by reductions in the cost of attendance. We therefore conclude that institutions and states themselves are likely to absorb a significant portion of the benefit of the tax cuts.

Whether such a transfer from the federal government to state governments and individual private institutions is desirable is a separate question. Although some private colleges and universities could increase their revenues significantly by adjusting their student aid calculations, the bulk of the transfer is likely to be public colleges and universities and state governments. This is mainly because that is where most of the students attend are, but also because these institutions will have incentives to raise prices and adjust their financial awarding policies.

Thus from one point of view, the tuition tax provisions can be seen as an intergovernmental transfer—a federal effort to relieve overstressed state budgets. Indeed, it is interesting that the projected federal revenue loss because of these tax cuts—averaging around $7 billion per year— is of the same order of magnitude as the reduction in real support of public higher education by state governments during the 1990s. President Clinton's program would to some extent relieve families of the additional financing burden generated by this reduction in state support but would also create an environment that encourages further reductions.

It is unlikely that those who advocated this course envisioned this result. In principle, a good case can be made for shifting the primary burden of government finance of higher education from the state to the federal level (a case we in fact made in *Keeping College Affordable*).[5] But at a time when budgetary resources are scarce at all levels of government, it seems desirable to design programs that encourage the state and federal governments to become partners in financing higher education, rather than programs that encourage one level of government to replace the efforts of another.

Trying to promote access to higher education through the tax system has other drawbacks. Tax benefits, for example, are of limited value in helping families who are strapped for cash to pay for college, because the relief comes late, when the tax form is submitted, rather than on the spot, as with grants and loans. Furthermore, there is every reason to expect that some providers of educational services will find ways to help families benefit from the tax breaks without providing the services the law intends.[6] Although the new legislation rules out tax breaks for "leisure-oriented" instruction, identifying and rooting out such instruction is a nightmare to contemplate and is bound to provoke outcry from those whose offerings are not deemed to qualify. Congress should remember the lessons learned from trying to control the participation of proprietary schools in the Guaranteed Student Loan program before creating a new program open to similar worries.

Perhaps our greatest reservation about tax subsidies for higher education is the opening of a channel by which revenue can flow through the tax system to subsidize college expenses. To us, this will open a new, steeper path that a revenue river can follow to the sea. We suspect that tax credits, once in the Code, will undergo broadening and deepening to allow favored constituencies to benefit more easily. Dollars headed for the tax side will grow over time and the traditional student aid programs, which are much better vehicles for providing access and choice, will gradually wither.

Furthermore, an underlying problem with tax credits is their influence on the need-based financial aid system. At best these tax benefits might be seen as neutral or indifferent toward the need-based approach, but in many ways they work to undercut need-based aid.

Tax credits compete for federal funds. As we have just noted, a crucial issue that Congress will regularly face in the future is whether to pour more money into popular though relatively ineffective tax breaks or to increase the resources available for Pell Grants and similar need-oriented programs. Tax credits also work against the need-based system by casting doubt on the principle that aid dollars from all sources should be carefully managed to target resources at those with limited ability to pay. Furthermore, tuition tax breaks give institutions and states incentives to cut back their own contributions to the need-based aid system. Tax breaks tend to shift the financing burden away from colleges and especially away from state governments in favor of the federal government. This is a far cry from organizing funding so that institutions, states, and the federal government view themselves as partners in addressing students' college financing needs.

AN ALTERNATIVE SPENDING APPROACH FOR NEW FEDERAL DOLLARS

An obvious alternative to tax incentives would be to spend equivalent amounts of revenue on expanding the Pell Grant program, perhaps in modified form. Senator Paul Wellstone (D-MN) last spring proposed raising the Pell Grant maximum to $5,000. A more modest program that would put the 1998-99 Pell Grant maximum at roughly its 1979-80 level would call for a $4,000 maximum Pell Grant Award. What would be the incentive effects of such a policy change and how much would it cost?

Clearly, increasing Pell Grant funding would provide low-cost public colleges with incentives to raise tuition. Such incentives are, however, attenuated by two important factors. First, unlike tax credits, which recognize only tuition as an educational cost, Pell Grant budgets reflect living expenses as well as tuition. Thus, even with a $4,000 or $5,000 maximum, relatively few institutions could qualify more students for aid by raising tuition. Moreover, again unlike tax credits, Pell Grants are designed to decline with increases in family income. Even with a higher maximum, relatively few students will be able to qualify for the larger awards associated with tuition increases because the award levels available to most students are well below the maximum.

Incentives for colleges to reduce their own student aid awards as Pell Grant awards increase are present, much as with tax credits. However, increased Pell Grants are much more likely to encourage greater numbers of relatively low-income, high-need students to attend college than would tax cuts. The presence of more such students would likely induce institutions and states to spend more of their own resources on student aid, thus at least partially—and conceivably more than fully—offsetting the tendency to substitute increased federal aid for state and institution-based resources.

There may be other ways for the federal government to become even more proactive in forging partnerships with states and institutions. The die is already cast on current tax legislation, but at some future point, when the federal government is ready to expand its contribution to financing higher education, it will be important to search for ways that encourage the other players in the system to maintain or even increase their own efforts.

Some approaches to this goal that have been proposed, while superficially attractive, have serious drawbacks. First, attempts by the federal government to mandate the behavior of state governments have been met with an increasingly chilly reception, generally for good reasons. Certainly the ability of the federal government to manage the pricing and aid decisions of states and individual colleges directly is minimal at best. Price controls or federal directives on the allocation of state- or institution-based aid as the cost of greater federal involvement in higher education would be an unworthy bargain and an imprudent line of march for the government.

A second tempting approach would be a program of federal matching grants for institution- or state-financed need-based aid. We might, for example, imagine a program supplemental to Pell Grants that contributed, say, $25 of federal grant money for every $100 of need-based grant money awarded to a student, above some threshold and up to the amount of the student's need. Such a program faces a very serious design problem, however. The amount of a student's need is a function of the institution's price. A college that raised its price and then used institutional grant money to discount the net price back to its former level would automatically qualify its students for more federal support. We have not been able to envision a bureaucratically manageable arrangement that overcomes this problem.

A variation on this kind of plan may, however, be worth considering. Suppose that instead of matching state or institutional spending on need-based aid, the federal government created a supplemental grant program that rewarded success in meeting the needs of low- and lower-middle-income students. Because greater need can be met either by lowering the price or by increasing need-based aid, this approach avoids the bias toward higher tuition implicit in the matching approach.

This is not the place to put forward a fully developed policy proposal for such an intervention. Any such design would need to attend to variations in the circumstances of different groups of students (e.g., adult students versus young people who depend on their parents for support) as well as of individual colleges and states. The following policy sketch may, however, usefully illustrate the possibilities.

Suppose that, rather than simply increasing the Pell Grant, the federal government introduced a new grant program "piggy-backed" on top of the Pell Grant program. These new grants would be means-tested, like the Pell Grant, but would also include a new institution-eligibility requirement. For a college's students to be eligible for the new "access" grants, the college would have to demonstrate that it met at least 90 percent of the financial need of all full-time, dependent, undergraduate students from families with incomes below $40,000 per year. Need would be calculated according to federal formulas and would be met by a combination of grants, loans, and work, with the amounts met by loans and work bounded by upper limits.

Such a grant program would have some desirable properties. For private institutions, it would ensure that significant institutional aid resources were being allocated to the neediest students. Setting the requirement at 90 percent of full need (or some other reasonable figure) would help discourage colleges from denying admission to high-need students to make the requirement easier to meet, without specifying the exact amount of aid each student is awarded.

For public institutions, this program would require one of two things. One option would be for a state to keep tuition at public institutions affordable enough so that low-income students' needs can be met through available resources. Alternatively, a state that chose to raise tuition (as many have done and likely will continue to do) would need to "recycle" enough of the added tuition dollars to keep college affordable for students from low-income families.

This approach, of course, raises complexities of its own. Deficiencies in the federal formula for calculating need are one such difficulty, although problems with the need-analysis formula tend to be less severe at the lower-income levels on which this program would focus. Moreover, an efficient and equitable way of dealing with part-time and independent students would not be easy to develop.

Another serious challenge is the need for fair treatment of institutions with widely varying levels of wealth (we are indebted to Sandy Baum of Skidmore College for emphasizing this point to us). It is relatively easy for heavily endowed institutions to meet the needs of their lower-income students (and many highly endowed institutions have a lower percentage of such students than those with smaller endowments). It is much more difficult for a poorly endowed institution to make a comparable effort. There is thus a risk that the proposed program would tend to exacerbate differences between the haves and the have-nots.

While recognizing this problem, it is also worth noting that institutions that are becoming increasingly involved in competitive discounting through student aid might be pleased with some of the incentives created by this program. If these colleges knew that they and their competitors had new incentives to concentrate their aid resources on relatively higher-need students, this might relieve some of the competitive pressures to provide more merit aid and other assistance to low-need applicants. The result could be aid programs that were more effective for the nation and more satisfying and appropriate for individual institutions.

Nonetheless, the problem of differential institutional resources needs to be dealt with. At a conceptual level, a couple of responses seem possible, although their practical feasibility needs further investigation. One possibility is to link eligibility for the "super-Pell Grant" program to relative award levels for students at different income levels as well as to some measure of overall success in meeting the needs of relatively low-income students. Thus an institution that met, say, 75 percent of need for students from families with incomes under $40,000 while devoting less than 10 percent of its aid budget to students from families with incomes over $75,000 might qualify. On the other hand, an institution that met 80 percent of low-income students' need but spent 40 percent of its aid budget on students from high-income families would not. Interestingly, this approach would actually encourage colleges to reduce tuition at the margin.

A second, perhaps more promising approach to this problem would be to link eligibility for the program to some measure of aid "effort" relative to available resources. There would be an analogy here to the way some states allocate funds to public school districts according to formulas that recognize the differential ability between districts to raise resources through property taxation. Imagine an effort index that related a college's success in meeting the needs of relatively low-income students to its endowment, current giving, and net tuition revenue levels. The debate over setting the parameters of such an effort formula would no doubt be lively, to say the least, but would also have the advantage of focusing attention on what colleges that receive federal support should be expected to do with their own resources.

The preceding discussion applies primarily to private colleges and universities. There are also differences between state governments in their ability to pay and in the portion of higher education services provided by state-run institutions. Taking state effort levels into account in defining program eligibility is certainly worth discussing. We would stress, however, that a fundamental rationale for public higher education is the goal of providing access to students from all economic backgrounds. We would not be inclined to cut state governments much slack in pursuing this goal as a test of their eligibility for such a program.

Many variations on the basic idea we have sketched here are of course feasible and worthy of discussion. Indeed, over the years, other analysts of higher education (including Arthur Hauptman and the late Fred Fischer) have put forward proposals aimed at encouraging states, colleges, and the federal government to work as partners. Realistic development of the program described here would require much further effort and significant political compromise. We would argue, however, that proposals on these lines, which recognize explicitly the need for partnerships between states, individual colleges, and the federal government, should be a prominent part of future discussions on federal higher education policy.

DEVISING NEW NATIONAL POLICIES

It is our opinion that those most likely to be placed at risk by the shifting environment of U.S. higher education are low-income students who do not have the strong qualifications needed for admission to selective private colleges. Equally at risk is the higher education system's goal of providing educational opportunity to qualified students from all economic backgrounds. As we argued above, for increasing numbers of students from low-income families, the only educational choice they can meaningfully consider is the local community college. Although this is a good alternative for many students, the choice of whether to attend a local community college, the flagship state university, or a high-cost private college should not be determined by accident of income and location but rather by aspiration and academic ability.

Cutbacks in state funding, which have produced increases in tuition charges at public institutions that have not been offset by increasing aid to needy students, play a large role in this constriction of opportunity. But a growing emphasis on merit aid at both public and private institutions and the increasing use of techniques such as "need-aware second review" that decrease the flow of institution-based aid to the neediest students have played a part as well. It is not reasonable to expect that individual colleges and universities, struggling with competitive pressures and funding limits, will find the strength to deal with these problems on their own.

At the same time, the capacities of both the state and federal governments will be strapped for the foreseeable future by limitations on their ability to raise revenue through taxation. In this environment we would stress the following considerations as critical to state and federal policies. For the states, it is essential in light of funding limitations that they focus their policies clearly on the fundamental purposes of a public university system. In the relative affluence of the 1960s, it was possible for states to conceive and partly execute ambitious "master plans," which found a place for everyone and provided generous subsidies to all who participated. In an era of greater perceived scarcity, the states should be more disciplined in focusing on the essential public purposes of their public colleges and universities. Foremost among these is offering an affordable choice of educational opportunities to students from all economic backgrounds. This purpose, we would argue, should take precedence over the goal of keeping the brightest students in the home state by offering large merit scholarships to high achievers or the goal of offering a deeply subsidized education to all students, including those from families with a substantial ability to pay.

The federal government, never the most important player in higher education from a financial point of view, has seen its role shrink under budgetary stringencies. More than ever, it must seek to maximize its leverage on the higher education system by using its limited resources intelligently.

First, the federal government must survey the whole higher education scene and concern itself with those matters that are most likely not to be attended to without its help. Most obviously, there is simply no reason for the federal government to get into the merit scholarship game, as President Clinton and various members of Congress have proposed doing. If one group of students in this country can be confident of gaining access to a suitable educational option at an affordable price, it is top-performing high school students. The explosion of merit aid through the individual actions of private and public colleges and universities provides significant incentives for many high school students. And if that were not enough, we must not forget that the system of selective admission already provides a powerful incentive for strong high school performance. For the federal government to gild that lily is a waste of both energy and resources.

Rather, high-need students lacking distinguished academic records are most likely to be neglected in the current higher education climate. This group is not a powerful constituency in most states, and private colleges and universities are increasingly reluctant to offer a large discount to a high-need student if they can recruit two comparable lower-need students for the same cost. The best tool available to the federal government for promoting the educational opportunities of this high-need group is well-targeted, means-tested student aid grants.

Second, many of the problems the federal government seems eager to address in higher education—help to students from middle-class families, merit awards for highly able students—are already being addressed by other parts of the system. The challenge of providing a range of good educational opportunities for high-need students is not being met.

The federal government must recognize that colleges and universities will react to the incentives its policies create rather than passively accepting their consequences. We discussed this issue previously, emphasizing in particular some of the worrisome incentive effects that may be created by offering tax credits for college. There is every reason to expect that both prices and financial aid practices would respond to such incentives in ways that would lead to the colleges themselves capturing a significant portion of the revenues provided by such credits. This, in our judgment, would not be a good outcome from a national point of view, and it is surely not the outcome envisioned by those who have advanced these proposals. To make this point is not at all to criticize colleges and universities for reacting in this way (if we are right about how they would react). As actors in a competitive system, it is both predictable and reasonable that they would adjust their policies to a changed fiscal environment.

We can, however, turn this second point around to a positive perspective. While avoiding the unintended consequences of the incentives it creates, the federal government should also seek to increase its leverage by taking into account the positive incentives its policies create. We believe that the program we have sketched here—providing new supplemental grant funds to students at colleges that meet the financial needs of their lower-income students—is a good example of the kinds of possibilities that should be pursued.

Third, while being realistic about the forces guiding both states and institutions, the federal government should also seek to identify situations in which those forces push states and institutions toward outcomes that are socially undesirable and try to offset those negative effects. Need-aware second review admission policies and the shift toward merit aid may make a good deal of sense for individual institutions, but they can exacerbate the disturbing trends in college access and choice. The considerable increases in tuition have led to a growing gap in enrollment rates between high- and low-income students and to an increased concentration of low-income students at the least costly institutions. With merit aid increasing at a faster rate than need-based aid, these trends seem likely to gain strength in the future.

CONCLUSION

So how should the federal government respond? The goal should be to keep the focus on need-based aid from eroding, both through direct federal action and by supporting the need-based dimension of state and institutional aid policies. This stance does not depend on a claim that the merit components of these policies should be rejected or actively discouraged by the federal government. Our claim, rather, is that the component of policy that needs to be sustained by the federal government is the need-based one. The federal government should actively fulfill its traditional role of providing aid to needy students. It should at the same time create incentives to push individual institutions to promote that goal as well. Earlier we outlined a new supplemental grant program that illustrates this kind of effort.

Increasing funding for the Pell Grant program is the most obvious way to ensure that low-income students will have both access to some type of postsecondary education and some reasonable choice between institutions. Indeed, increases in means-tested student aid should receive the highest priority for federal funding in higher education. Furthermore, as we noted earlier, there is some empirical evidence that providing more federal need-based aid encourages increased aid expenditures by institutions from their own resources. While President Clinton has consistently called for an increase in the maximum Pell Grant, there is little hope of finding enough resources to restore earlier levels of real funding to the Pell Grant program.

Federal dollars to support students' efforts to get a college education are, and will be, very scarce. We must do our utmost to use those precious dollars well. On this, the twenty-fifth anniversary of the Pell Grant, we believe the nation should rededicate itself to developing a financial aid program that offers more direct benefits to the students for whom the issue of college affordability is the most pressing.

MICHAEL S. MCPHERSON *is president of Macalester College. From 1994 to 1996 he was dean of the faculty at Williams College and earlier served as chair of the Williams Economics Department. McPherson has written widely on the ethics and economics of higher education. He is coauthor of* Keeping College Affordable: Government and Educational Opportunity. *His new book,* The Student Aid Game: Meeting Need and Rewarding Talent in American Higher Education, *coauthored with Morton Schapiro, was published by Princeton University Press in fall 1997.*

MORTON OWEN SCHAPIRO *is professor of economics and dean of the University of Southern California's College of Letters, Arts, and Sciences. He was previously chair of USC's Department of Economics. Schapiro is an authority on college financing and affordability and on trends in education costs and student aid. He is author or coauthor of five books, including (with Michael S. McPherson)* Keeping College Affordable *and* The Student Aid Game.

NOTES

1. Michael S. McPherson and Morton Owen Schapiro, *The Student Aid Game: Meeting Need and Rewarding Talent in American Higher Education* (Princeton, N.J.: Princeton University Press, 1997).
2. Thomas J. Kane, "Rising Public College Tuition and College Entry: How Well Do Public Subsidies Promote Access to College?" National Bureau of Economic Research Working Paper No. 5164, July 1995.
3. See David Breneman, "Statement to the Committee on Ways and Means, U.S. House of Representatives," Testimony at the Hearing on Education and Training Tax Provisions of the Administration's Fiscal Year 1998 Budget Proposal, March 5, 1997.
4. Michael S. McPherson and Morton Owen Schapiro, *Keeping College Affordable: Government and Educational Opportunity* (Washington, D.C.: Brookings Institution, 1991).
5. Ibid.
6. See Thomas J. Kane, "Beyond Tax Relief: Long-term Challenges in Financing Higher Education," Testimony before the Committee on Ways and Means, U.S. House of Representatives, at the Hearing on Education and Training Tax Provisions of the Administration's Fiscal Year 1998 Budget Proposal, March 5, 1997.

Afterword

Lawrence E. Gladieux

The Twenty-Fifth Anniversary Pell Grant Conference in November 1997 coincided with President Clinton's signing into law the appropriation bill that raised the Pell Grant maximum to $3,000 in academic year 1998-99. This increase was part of a broad federal budget agreement between Congress and the president. In an effort to balance his tuition tax relief proposals, which would primarily benefit middle- and upper-middle-income families, President Clinton insisted on the increase for Pell Grants to help low-income students and families.

As we move into the next century, however, it is unclear whether need-based financial aid will be sustained as the principal federal strategy to equalize postsecondary opportunities. A frequent refrain at the Twenty-Fifth Anniversary Pell Grant Conference, echoed in several chapters of this book, was that we have only begun to scratch the surface of the ramifications of the Taxpayer Relief Act of 1997 for the future financing of higher education and the federal role in helping students and families to pay college costs.

The federal government now has two ways of delivering college financial assistance, one through the tax code and one through direct appropriation. The two sets of benefits operate on different principles and serve different, though overlapping, populations. In general, under the tax code, the more income one has (up to the income ceilings established in the law), the more one benefits. Under the need-based aid programs, the less income one has, the more one benefits. And again in general, the tuition tax benefits will go primarily to students and families with incomes above the median, while most Pell Grants and other need-tested assistance go to families below the median.

While the recent funding boost for Pell Grants restores some of the purchasing power lost in this program since the 1970s, there remains a long way to go. Like other discretionary programs, Pell Grants have no guaranteed financing from year to year, and further real increases will not come easily under prevailing budget rules and agreements. In contrast, the tuition tax breaks function, in effect, as an entitlement not tied to annual appropriations, and history suggests that once such benefits are written into the tax code, there will be persistent pressure over time to expand eligibility for them.

Over the long haul, how will these two sets of benefits interact? Which will predominate? How will the federal government deliver the bulk of its assistance to students and families for paying postsecondary costs—through the tax code or through Title IV of the Higher Education Act? The jury is out on these and other questions about the impact of the new tuition tax provisions—on federal policy as well as state and institutional tuition and aid decisions.

Meanwhile, the goal of equalizing college opportunities remains as important today as when the Higher Education Act was passed in 1965 or the Pell Grant program was created in 1972. In fact, postsecondary education is more important than ever, to the individual and to society. Forces running deep in our economy have ratcheted up skill and credential requirements in the job market, putting a premium on education beyond high school. Estimates vary from 70 to 90 percent on the proportion of future jobs that will require postsecondary training, and the demand for skills shows no signs of abating.

Yet postsecondary opportunities remain unequal across society, wage and wealth disparities have reached unprecedented extremes, and the least educated and skilled are left further and further behind. Federal higher education policy has traditionally focused on helping those most at-risk, and now is not the time to erode that fundamental commitment.

To close gaps in opportunity and meet our society's need for a skilled and competitive workforce, financial aid is more important than ever — aid that is generally targeted to students with the fewest resources and delivered to students and families as simply and predictably as possible. As McPherson and Schapiro suggest, we need somehow to rekindle the commitment to need-based principles that inspired the original Pell Grant, and we need to restore a sense of partnership among the federal government, states, and institutions in helping the neediest students to go to college.

A clear message from the Twenty-Fifth Anniversary Conference was that we also need more research on the significant but elusive effects of Pell Grants and other means-tested aid. Sarah Turner has documented for us a number of unforeseen results. John Lee has gauged the Pell Grant's contribution to student persistence in college. And Tony Carnevale and Lou Jacobson tell us about the Pell Grant's quiet but substantial role in workforce training and retraining of at-risk adults. These findings are helpful. Yet we are still straining to know what we need to know in order to make the most successful advocacy for Pell Grants, both absolutely and in combination with other types of aid.

Ultimately, however, financial aid is not enough. To equalize college opportunities, we need more fundamental, complementary strategies. We need intervention in human lives, and we need to focus on student success, not just access—persistence to degree, not just getting students in the door.

The problem of unequal opportunity has proved more intractable than anyone anticipated when the Pell Grant was created 25 years ago. Perhaps we expected too much of financial aid. Tuition and aid policies are extremely important, but access to higher education is not just a financial issue. Even if we could get a $5,000 Pell Grant maximum, as Senator Paul Wellstone has in fact proposed, there is much else that needs to be done.

Above all, we need a much wider and deeper societal commitment to reaching, motivating, and preparing at-risk students. In fact, the data tell us that academic preparation overrides just about everything else in determining who goes to college and where, and who gets a degree.

This may have been the most important theme of the Twenty-Fifth Anniversary Conference—that Pell Grants and other financial aid alone cannot do the job. As Arnold Mitchem said in his remarks, "We need to tie dollars to aspirations." Martin Kramer invokes the early vision of Pell Grants to remind us that motivation and preparation are critical to equalizing opportunity. Arthur Hauptman sends the same message in urging public policymakers to try to replicate the success of private early-intervention programs. And Sam Kipp's analysis of the coming generation underscores that postsecondary opportunity for the new students will depend not just on removing financial barriers but preparing them for college-level work.

Representative Chaka Fattah, a former Pell Grant recipient and now a second-term congressman from Philadelphia, spoke at the conference about his proposed Twenty-First Century Scholars Program. The congressman's program would provide mentoring and early notice of college aid to sixth-grade students who live in communities with high rates of poverty. A scaled-down version of his legislation is likely to be included in the 1998 reauthorization of the Higher Education Act.

The point is that there are "I Have a Dream" and scores of similar programs out there that reach and motivate at-risk students (and often involve their parents), build self-esteem and a sense of possibility for the future, and encourage students to study hard and achieve their goals. With the right counseling, support, and role models, these programs can and do work. The problem is that for the millions of youngsters whose life chances are dim and might be lifted by an "I Have a Dream" or similar program, the movement is almost like a wheel of fortune. A youngster must be lucky enough to be in the right city, the right school, and the right classroom at the right time.

The challenge for public policy is to leverage these efforts to a much larger scale.

Pell Grants may not have lived up to the vision of a universal GI Bill, but they *have* made a big difference. They can make *more* of a difference if we all do our homework, think creatively, and above all, work together, so that a quarter century from now—on the fiftieth anniversary of Pell Grants—we will have even more to celebrate than we do today.

Appendix:
Speakers, Panelists, and Participants

TWENTY-FIFTH ANNIVERSARY PELL GRANT CONFERENCE
NOVEMBER 13 AND 14, 1997

Forum One: Memory

OPENING REMARKS

Donald M. Stewart
President, The College Board

PANEL A

Lawrence E. Gladieux
*Executive Director, Policy Analysis,
The College Board*

Thomas R. Wolanin
*Research Professor, George Washington
University
Senior Associate, The Institute for
Higher Education Policy*

Martin A. Kramer
Consultant, Berkeley, California

Lois D. Rice,
*Guest Scholar
The Brookings Institution*

PANEL B

John B. Childers
*Vice President, Government
Relations and Communications,
The College Board*

Robert Shireman
*Senior Policy Advisor,
The White House*

Arnold L. Mitchem
*Executive Director, National Council of
Educational Opportunity Associations*

Victor Klatt
*Coordinator for Education Policy,
House Education and the Workforce
Committee*

Gala Dinner: A Celebration

MASTER OF CEREMONIES

The Honorable Pat Williams
Former U.S. Representative, Montana

STATEMENTS BY PELL GRANT
RECIPIENTS

Nathan Ambrose
Union College

Angela Neal
Austin Peay State University

Anthony Samu
United States Student Association

Eileen Withey
Sky Tel Corporation

TRIBUTES TO SENATOR PELL

The Honorable Richard W. Riley
U.S. Secretary of Education

The Honorable Tom Eagleton
Former U.S. Senator, Missouri

The Honorable Augustus F. Hawkins
Former U.S. Representative, California

The Honorable Christopher J. Dodd
U.S. Senator, Connecticut

The Honorable James M. Jeffords
U.S. Senator, Vermont

The Honorable Jack Reed
U.S. Senator, Rhode Island

The Honorable Ted Stevens
U.S. Senator, Alaska

The Honorable Robert A. Weygand
*U.S. House Representative, Rhode
Island*

Forum Two: Reason

REMARKS

Barry McCarty
Dean of Enrollment Services, Lafayette College

The Honorable Chaka Fattah
U.S. House Representative, Pennsylvania

PANEL A

Watson Scott Swail
Associate Director, Policy Analysis, The College Board

Sarah E. Turner
Assistant Professor, Policy Studies and Economics, University of Virginia

John B. Lee
President, JBL Associates, Inc.

Anthony P. Carnevale
Vice President, Public Leadership, Educational Testing Service

PANEL B

Thomas Parker
Senior Vice President, The Education Resources Institute

W. Lee Hansen
Professor of Economics, University of Wisconsin at Madison

Catherine C. Thomas
Associate Dean, Admissions and Financial Aid, University of Southern California

Philip R. Day, Jr.
President, Daytona Beach Community College

David Evans
Legislative Associate House Committee on Education and the Workforce

Forum Three: Imagination

REMARKS

Arnold L. Mitchem
Executive Director, National Council of Educational Opportunity Associations

David L. Warren
President, National Association of Independent Colleges and Universities

Stanley O. Ikenberry
President, American Council on Education

PANEL

Rev. William J. Byron
Professor of Management, Georgetown University

Samuel M. Kipp III
President, Kipp Research and Consulting

Arthur M. Hauptman
Consultant, Arlington, Virginia

Michael S. McPherson
President, Macalester College

Morton Owen Schapiro
Professor of Economics and Dean, University of Southern California

CLOSING REMARKS

Lawrence E. Gladieux
Executive Director, Policy Analysis, The College Board

TWENTY-FIFTH ANNIVERSARY PELL GRANT
CONFERENCE PARTICIPANTS
NOVEMBER 13 AND 14, 1997

Barbara Abrams
Cornell University

Erica Adelsheimer
United States Student Association

Ronald Allan
Georgetown University

Sister M. Therese Antone, RSM
Salve Regina University

Bart Astor
The College Board

David Baime
American Association of Community Colleges

Beverly A. Beard
The College Board

Anthony J. Bellia
Canisius College

Barbara Bennison
California State University

David Bergeron
U.S. Department of Education

Lexy Boudreau
National Council of Educational Opportunity Associations

Pamela A. Britton
Southern Illinois University at Carbondale

John F. Brugel
Rutgers University

Maureen Budetti
National Association of Independent Colleges and Universities

John F. Burness
Duke University

Thomas Butts
University of Michigan

Benjamin V. Cabell

Alberto F. Cabrera
The Pennsylvania State University

Susan Cameron
Former Appointment Secretary to Senator Pell

Michael D. Carr
The Widmeyer Baker Group, Inc.

Steve Carter
U.S. Department of Education

Robert Caruano
The College Board

Conwey Casillas
Education Finance Council, Inc.

Constance Clark
The College Board-Upward Bound Program

Gay Clyburn
American Association of State Colleges and Universities

Ann Coles
The Education Resources Institute

Kristin D. Conklin
The National Center for Public Policy and Higher Education

Carla Craddock
The College Fund/UNCF

Winkie Crigler
Williams and Jensen

Dolores Cross
GE Fund

Evelyn Dávila-Blackburn
The College Board

Christopher Davis
National Council of Educational Opportunity Associations

Jerry Davis
Sallie Mae, Inc.

Jan Demers
Assistant to Senator Claiborne Pell

Fred Dietrich
The College Board

Kate Dillon
Arizona State University

Humphrey Doermann
Macalester College

Lawrence Dolan
The College Board-EQUITY 2000®

Joseph Drew
Southeastern University

Brother Patrick Ellis, FSC
Catholic University of America

Edward M. Elmendorf
American Association of State Colleges and Universities

Melanie Esten
National Association of Independent Colleges and Universities

Jerrye Brown Feliciana
Howard University

Robert H. Fenske
Arizona State University

Rodney Ferguson
The Widmeyer Baker Group, Inc.

Brian K. Fitzgerald
Advisory Committee on Student Financial Assistance

Sarah Flanagan
National Association of Independent Colleges and Universities

Ernest T. Freeman
The Education Resources Institute

Jean S. Frohlicher
National Council of Higher Education Loan Programs

Gregory Fusco
Fusco Associates

Antoine M. Garibaldi
Howard University

Stephanie Giesecke
Association of Community College Trustees

Dolores Gomez
National Council of Educational Opportunity Associations

Ruth Granados
National Association for College Admission Counseling

Sarita Gupta
United States Student Association

Janetta Hammock
Higher Education & National Affairs

William D. Hansen
Education Finance Council, Inc.

Stephanie Harris
Student Lending Update

James C. Hearn
University of Georgia

Hal Higginbotham
The College Board

John T. Hill
U.S. Department of Education

The Honorable Ruben Hinojosa
U.S. House of Representatives

Howard E. Holcomb
Council of Independent Colleges

Maureen Hoyler
National Council of Educational Opportunity Associations

Thomas G. Hughes
Former Chief of Staff for Senator Claiborne Pell

Robert Igbinovia
Educational Opportunity Program-NJIT

Earl G. Ingram
George Mason University

Louis Jacobson
WESTAT, Inc.

Richard T. Jerue
Education Management Corporation

Barbara Jones
Howard University

Pallavi Kearney
The College Board

Barrie J. Kelly
The College Board

Christopher M. Kiernan
Salve Regina University

The Honorable Dale E. Kildee
U.S. House of Representatives

Jacqueline King
American Council on Education

Sally K. Kirkgasler
U.S. Department of Education

Jeffrey Kittay
Lingua Franca

Paula Kuebler
The College Board-EQUITY 2000

Christopher Labonte
Office of Representative Robert Weygand

Moira Lennehan
McA Enterprises, Inc.

Audrey Lesesne
Office of Representative Mike McIntyre

Marty LeVor
The LeVor Group

Kathleen Little
The College Board

Cyndy Littlefield
Association of Jesuit Colleges & Universities

Jennifer Lockhart
GE Fund

David A. Longanecker
U.S. Department of Education

Andrew G. Malizio
National Center for Education Statistics

Philecia McCain
Office of Representative Chaka Fattah

Joe McCormick
U.S. Department of Education

Katie McGraw
National Council of Educational Opportunity Associations

The Honorable Mike McIntyre
U.S. House of Representatives

Maureen McLaughlin
U.S. Department of Education

Patricia McWade
Georgetown University

Frank Mensel
American Student Association of Community Colleges

Jamie P. Merisotis
Institute for Higher Education Policy

Dana Mikelson
The College Board

Roy Millenson
Former U.S. Senate Committee Staff

Paulette Morgan
The College Board-EOC

Thomas Mortenson
Postsecondary Education OPPORTUNITY

Walter H. Moulton
Bowdoin College

Tom Netting
Career College Association

Sherry A. Newton
The College Fund/UNCF

Julius Nimmons, Jr.
University of the District of Columbia

Ellin Nolan
Dean, Blakey & Moskowitz

The Honorable
Eleanor Holmes Norton
U.S. House of Representatives

Luis Ocasio
Hispanic Association of Colleges and Universities

Lawrence F. Padberg
Marymount University

Rose Mary Padberg
Marymount University

John Parker
Drake University

Willis Parker
Southeastern University

Glenda Partee
American Youth Policy Forum

Jeffrey Penn
The College Board

Kent Phillippe
American Association of Community Colleges

Al Phillips
National Council of Educational Opportunity Associations

John Phillips
Higher Educational Management Group, Ltd.

Catherine Pohlman
The College Board

The Honorable John Edward Porter
U.S. House of Representatives

Duane Quinn
American Student Assistance

Paul Ramsey
Educational Testing Service

Kenneth W. Rodgers
The College Board

The Honorable Tim Roemer
U.S. House of Representatives

Teri Rucker
American Association of Community Colleges

Thomas Rudin
The College Board

Reggie Sanders
The College Board-EQUITY 2000

Edward Santos
College Board Student Representative

Jennifer Sarnelli
The College Board

William M. Schilling
University of Pennsylvania

The Honorable Robert C. Scott
U.S. House of Representatives

Lydia Sermons
Office of Representative Chaka Fattah

Dorothy Sexton
The College Board

Linda Shiller
Vermont Student Assistance Corporation

Rolin Sidwell
Office of Policy and Evaluation, District of Columbia

Chris Simmons
National Commission on the Cost of Higher Education

Richard T. Sonnergren
Former U.S. Department of Education Official

Irene Spero
The College Board

Jacob O. Stampen
University of Wisconsin-Madison

Rachael Sternberg
U.S. Department of Education

Roberta Merchant-Stoutamire
The College Board

Eustace Theodore
Council for the Advancement and Support of Education

Barbara E. Tornow
Boston University

Mark Traversa
U.S. Department of Education

Johnny Villamil
The ASPIRA Association, Inc.

Omer Waddles
Career College Association

Steve Wallace
The Pennsylvania State University

Sue Watts
The College Board

Nan S. Wells
Princeton University

Karen Wilcox
Massachusetts Institute of Technology

Kevin Wilson
Office of Representative Robert Weygand

Elaine Zimmerman
Department of Education

Brian Zucker
Human Capital Research Corporation